THE EQUATION

Finding Peace Through the Storm

Rob and Lisa Laizure

The Equation
Finding Peace Through the Storm

By Rob & Lisa Laizure

Printed in the United States

ISBN 978-0-9832997-8-3

ConnectingTheDotsMinistries.com

Table of Contents

The Equation

Chapter 1

Your Past

Life is filled with storms. When the skies become dark, the wind starts howling and the rain begins pouring - we all have a choice. We can choose to stand in the storm unprotected or we can run for cover. Life is also like that. As the storms of life come upon us - impending divorce, loss of a loved one, addiction, or physical illness - we can let these unpleasant circumstances affect us or we can seek shelter and live out the storm under God's protection and in peace.

In this book we will meet a man named Joseph who went through storm after storm in his life. But instead of standing in the midst of the squall he learned how to seek shelter in his God. And when he did, he learned that through all his problems he could find the peace he needed to continue on.

As we begin, imagine yourself being the pampered child in your family where the majority of your siblings despise you. Your brothers hate you enough to sell you as a slave and send you far away from your doting father. You find yourself alone in a foreign country where you are falsely accused and thrown into prison for years and years. You are confused, hurt and angry. What would you do? How would you handle the rest of your life knowing how devastating your past has been?

Maybe you have felt this kind of betrayal in your life to some degree. Possibly you were fired from a job or your spouse walked out on you. Perhaps someone stole from you or lied to you. Maybe you were abused as a child or accused of something you did not do. Where do you go from here?

A few summers ago, someone close to us was experiencing this same kind of pain. It wasn't slavery or prison but it was betrayal, deception and lies. As we watched the heartbreak unfold, our first instinct was to be angry. We wanted to get involved. We wanted to help lessen the pain. Our desire was to defend the person we cared for who was being hurt.

And yet...
We couldn't.

It was then we realized how important a simple math equation we learned in childhood would help change the course of how we were feeling. One of the first things we learned in school was simple math:

1 +1 = 2
and
1 +1 +1 = 3.

It was the last equation that made life bearable and acceptable once again.

This is how it looked for us:

Me + problem =
FRUSTRATION (hurt, anger, pain, unforgiveness)

Me + problem + God =
PEACE (tranquility, harmony, reconciliation)

Somehow when we posed this problem in a different equation it changed the entire outcome. Now instead of being disappointed and saddened at the situation, we became hopeful and peaceful knowing the God who controlled it all was still involved. It still didn't make sense and we couldn't begin to see the whole picture but it renewed our hearts knowing that ***with Him in the equation*** – the answer to the problem would come out better than we ever expected. Without inserting God into the problem, we would be different people.

We would be bitter and unforgiving.

We would be angry and spiteful.

We would want revenge and retaliation.

But...by putting God into the situation the answer we come up with is peace. Peace because as we see His hand in all that happens in life – good or bad – we can trust He has a purpose behind it all.

How do we get there? How do we put God in the equation when our world is falling apart? How is it possible to go through difficult days and yet still have peace and joy? The answer to this problem will be found in the one place that has all the answers: the Bible. God has given us His Word as a manual for life. He has given us this incredible Book to show us how to make it through the difficult days ahead, to help us deal with the complications and heartaches that happen to all of us.

The Bible is where we find Joseph who had been through more hopeless situations and despair than most of us will ever know and yet he lived his life doing one thing. He always added God into his equation. Because he did, he was able to live his life with a different perspective than most people around him. For us, thousands of years later, Joseph is the perfect example for us to follow. He refused to let his negative circumstances destroy his life or his peace because with God in the equation he knew there was always a purpose to his pain.

We find Joseph in **Genesis 37:1-4 Now Jacob lived in the land where his father had sojourned, in the land of Canaan. These are the records of the generations of Jacob. Joseph, when seventeen years of age, was pasturing the flock with his brothers while he was still a youth, along with the sons of Bilhah and the sons of Zilpah, his father's wives. And Joseph brought back a bad report about them to their father. Now Israel loved Joseph more than all his sons, because he was the son of his old age; and he made him a varicolored tunic. His brothers saw that their father loved him more than all his brothers; and so they hated him and could not speak to him on friendly terms.**

To begin with, we need a little history about Joseph's father Jacob. Jacob fell in love with a woman, Rachel. Jacob promised her father Laban that he would work for him seven years in order to marry her and yet on their wedding night, Laban tricked Jacob into marrying Rachel's sister Leah since Leah was older. He then made a deal with Jacob to work an additional seven years for Rachel who was the one he wanted to marry in the first place.

All of this drama presented serious problems for Jacob. He now had two wives who were sisters – and Rachel, the one he loved, was barren and could not get pregnant.

Leah on the other hand seemed to be pregnant all the time and so Rachael decided to get her maid involved in hopes of having children through her. Leah decided to do the same and so between the maids and Leah – ten children were born.

Genesis 30:22-24 tells us that finally, God opened Rachel's womb.

> **"Then God remembered Rachel, and God gave heed to her and opened her womb. So she conceived and bore a son and said, "God has taken away my reproach." She named him Joseph, saying, "May the Lord give me another son."**

God gave Rachel a son, Joseph, and soon after became pregnant again. As they were traveling, Rachel went into labor and gave birth to her second son, Benjamin, but she ended up dying in the process.

> **Genesis 35:15-18 So Jacob named the place where God had spoken with him, Bethel. Then they journeyed from Bethel; and when there was still some distance to go to Ephrath, Rachel began to give birth and she suffered severe labor. When she was in severe labor the midwife said to her, "Do not fear, for now you have another son." It came about as her soul was departing (for she died), that she named him Ben-oni; but his father called him Benjamin.**

Jacob ended up with twelve sons, two who were born to him by the love of his life Rachel. That was where the problems started. Jacob made it clear to the older boys that Joseph and Benjamin were his favorites. One lesson to be learned from this story is the importance of treating all of our children the same and making sure we do not have favorites. This became an incredibly dysfunctional family because Jacob did not make it clear to all his children that he loved them equally.

As we begin the story of Joseph we have to remember what **Genesis 30:22** said: **"God opened her womb."** For Rachel, God should have been added into the equation of her inability to get pregnant. Her life would have been completely different had she recognized God behind her seemingly hopeless situation. Unfortunately because she didn't, Rachel's life was one of jealousy, frustration, anger, and resentment and she could not see the whole picture. She had no idea that the reason God did not allow her to get pregnant was because someday the nation of Israel would be in trouble and her son Joseph, who was not born yet, would be used by God to save the day. She focused on today without regard for the future.

Think how her life would have been different if she had added God into her frustrating equation. Think of the turmoil her life produced because she forgot to say "God, I don't like this. This is not fair. My sister gets all the babies and I am left with heartache ***and yet*** knowing You are in this equation, I will trust that YOU have a plan beyond anything I can see at the moment." As we look back on the life of Joseph we can see in hindsight that God did have a plan – just as He has one for your life today.

Take the time to stop and think about what it is in your life that is stressing you out. Maybe it is:

Bankruptcy
Wanting a baby
Wayward children
Sickness
Fearful of the future
Marital problems
Singleness
Work issues

Whatever you are struggling with, take a look back at the story of Joseph. His life had God's hand on it even before Jacob fell in love with Rachel. She didn't see it then and regardless of whether we see it or not – the fact is that God has a plan and we are part of it. There is purpose in financial problems, barrenness, singleness, and heartache. There is intention on the part of God where you are in your life right now. Do not let the problems of this life cloud the picture: God has a purpose for all you are going through.

One definition we found for the word "purpose" is this:

Purpose: The reason for which something is done or created or for which something exists.

As a child of God, we have to go through life knowing He has reasons for what is happening in our lives. He has a purpose for us being born. We were created by Him by design. We were not accidents – there was intention on His part when creating us. We have seven children and the last two showed up, unplanned, when our youngest at the time was eight years old. We were told we could not have any more children so when we heard Lisa was pregnant we were shocked. Our youngest daughter asked us one day if she was an "accident" which we replied – "there are no accidents when it comes to God." She may not have been planned by us but we know she was planned by God and because of that, we are convinced He will use her in mighty ways.

When we think of His purposes, we have to remember that as He is moving us to the place where we need to be, sometimes that journey is difficult. But, inserting God into the equation will give us a different perspective. As we see how Joseph's life began we see that regardless of his past or how he was raised as a child, this did not affect God's plans in any way. If you have had a complicated life thus far – embrace it. Know that God can use you regardless of your past.

As we end this chapter we cannot move on until we explain the most important part of your life: Jesus. The Bible is clear that in **Romans 8:28** we are assured of this: **And we know that God causes all things to work together for good to those who love God, to those who are called according to His purpose.** God promises to work all things – even the problems of your life – together for good to those who know Him. That means to those who have a personal relationship with God through His Son Jesus. **John 14:6** explains: **Jesus said to him, "I am the way, and the truth, and the life; no one comes to the Father but through Me.**

There is only one way to God and that is through His son Jesus. He is the only way to know God and to spend eternity in heaven. He is the answer to your fear and frustrations in life. He is the answer to wondering about the reason for living. The minute you ask Him to come into your life you can know with certainty that "all things work together for good."

Knowing Jesus brings peace into our lives. Knowing Jesus brings calmness and quietness in the midst of turmoil. As we study the life of Joseph, we recognize that somehow he understood the principle of always including God in the equations of his life. Because of that, he viewed his problems as being under the umbrella of God's sovereignty and control, which is what we are challenged to do in our own lives. Look at your past with a different lens. Nothing surprises Him. He has a purpose. Move forward with that knowledge.

Chapter 2

When Life Changes

When Joseph was seventeen he was branded by his brothers as their father's "favorite." They hated the fact their father doted on Joseph, gave him a special coat and loved him more than them. While all his brothers were pasturing the flock one day, Joseph ran back to his father and told him all the things his brothers were doing. Because of this, his brothers despised him.

In the Old Testament, God spoke to people in many different ways. Sometimes He communicated through dreams and visions. One day, Joseph had a dream from God which he decided to share with his entire family. Unfortunately, what he thought was exciting, did not set very well with his siblings who ended up hating him more than they already did.

> **Genesis 37:5-11 Then Joseph had a dream, and when he told it to his brothers, they hated him even more. He said to them, "Please listen to this dream which I have had; for behold, we were binding sheaves in the field, and lo, my sheaf rose up and also stood erect; and behold, your sheaves gathered around and bowed down to my sheaf." Then his brothers said to him, "Are you actually going to reign over us? Or are you really going to rule over us?" So they**

hated him even more for his dreams and for his words. Now he had still another dream, and related it to his brothers, and said, "Lo, I have had still another dream; and behold, the sun and the moon and eleven stars were bowing down to me." He related it to his father and to his brothers; and his father rebuked him and said to him, "What is this dream that you have had? Shall I and your mother and your brothers actually come to bow ourselves down before you to the ground?" His brothers were jealous of him, but his father kept the saying in mind.

Whether Joseph was bragging about his dream or excited for what he felt God told him, this news did nothing but make his brothers despise him even more. Joseph, had two dreams, both of which alluded to the fact that his family would bow down to him. His brothers were furious and jealous and the two feelings mixed together produced a chain of events that would dramatically change all of their lives.

The sad part of this story is how bitterness and anger toward another person can destroy a life. Our time on earth is short compared to eternity and yet years are often wasted by animosity toward someone who has hurt us. It is amazing how the root of our hatred hurts us the most but even more how it affects our future. God wants us to live a life of peace regardless of our circumstances and yet what holds many of us back is ill will toward others.

What we need to learn from Joseph's brothers is that when a difficult person comes into our life we always have a choice: get by it or let it destroy us. The problem is we live in a world that says we have rights. We don't have to take abuse from anyone. We should be able to get back at the person who is hurting us. Yet as a follower of Jesus, we never have that option. As followers of Jesus our goal in life is to look more and more like Him. Paul talks about this in Philippians:

> **Philippians 2:3-8 "Do nothing from selfishness or empty conceit, but with humility of mind regard one another as more important than yourselves; do not merely look out for your own personal interests, but also for the interests of others. Have this attitude in yourselves which was also in Christ Jesus, who, although He existed in the form of God, did not regard equality with God a thing to be grasped, but emptied Himself, taking the form of a bond-servant, and being made in the likeness of men. Being found in appearance as a man, He humbled Himself by becoming obedient to the point of death, even death on a cross."**

And with these words we are told what our job is when people hurt us. We are to regard them as more important. We are to look out for their interests. Think about Jesus. He left heaven and humbled Himself on earth. People mocked Him, spit on Him, shoved a crown of thorns on His head and crucified Him on a cross. But what if He claimed His rights or got back at those who hurt Him? What if He became bitter at those who were wounding Him? What if He hopped off the cross and destroyed every person who put Him there?

What we learn is that people meant more to Jesus than Him demanding His own rights. And that is what we have to learn as His followers. Think of the different outcome in the life of Joseph's brothers if they had done what Jesus did. What would have happened if they had prayed for Joseph rather than hated him? What would have happened if they prayed for their own attitudes - that God would give them a love for their brother? What if their focus was upward toward the things of God instead of inward on themselves? Think of the different lives these men would have lived had they looked within themselves to change rather than letting their jealousy and bitterness take root in their lives.

> **Genesis 37:12-17 Then his brothers went to pasture their father's flock in Shechem. Israel said to Joseph, "Are not your brothers pasturing the flock in Shechem? Come, and I will send you to them." And he said to him, "I will go." Then he said to him, "Go now and see about the welfare of your brothers and the welfare of the flock, and bring word back to me." So he sent him from the valley of Hebron, and he came to Shechem. A man found him, and behold, he was wandering in the field; and the man asked him, "What are you looking for?" He said, "I am looking for my brothers; please tell me where they are pasturing the flock." Then the man said, "They have moved from here; for I heard them say, 'Let us go to Dothan.' " So Joseph went after his brothers and found them at Dothan.**

In a way we can see how frustrated Joseph's brothers were. It was Joseph's job to go out to the field and see what his brothers were doing with the flocks and report back to his dad. Understandably, his brothers loathed him but on this particular day it was different. They were done with Joseph and wanted to make sure he would no longer be around, so they decided to hatch a plan.

> **Genesis 37:18 When they saw him from a distance and before he came close to them, they plotted against him to put him to death. They said to one another, "Here comes this dreamer! "Now then, come and let us kill him and throw him into one of the pits; and we will say, 'A wild beast devoured him.' Then let us see what will become of his dreams!" But Reuben heard this and rescued him out of their hands and said, "Let us not take his life." Reuben further said to them, "Shed no blood. Throw him into this pit that is in the wilderness, but do not lay hands on him"—that he might rescue him out of their hands, to restore him to his father.**

Reuben was the oldest and probably the wisest at this point. He recognized that murder was not something he wanted to be involved with. He knew how much his father loved Joseph but even as annoying as Joseph was, he was confident his father's heart would be broken if his favorite son was dead. Reuben wanted no part of this so he left for a while, which was long enough to be gone when his brothers came up with a different plan.

> **Genesis 37:23 So it came about, when Joseph reached his brothers, that they stripped Joseph of his tunic, the varicolored tunic that was on him; and they took him and threw him into the pit. Now the pit was empty, without any water in it. Then they sat down to eat a meal. And as they raised their eyes and looked, behold, a caravan of Ishmaelites was coming from**

> **Gilead, with their camels bearing aromatic gum and balm and myrrh, on their way to bring them down to Egypt. Judah said to his brothers, "What profit is it for us to kill our brother and cover up his blood? "Come and let us sell him to the Ishmaelites and not lay our hands on him, for he is our brother, our own flesh." And his brothers listened to him. Then some Midianite traders passed by, so they pulled him up and lifted Joseph out of the pit, and sold him to the Ishmaelites for twenty shekels of silver. Thus they brought Joseph into Egypt.**

The plan they decided on was to sell Joseph to traders and let them take him far away to Egypt where he would be forced to work for someone as a slave. That way, Joseph's death would not be on the brothers. He would be alive but out of their lives. They figured that once he was gone on the wagon to Egypt, Joseph wouldn't be their problem anymore.

Many times when we walk away from difficult circumstances or challenging people we assume our lives will be better. We see marriages falling apart and people walking out on their spouse in hopes of an easier life. We watch children leave home because they hate their parent's authority. We see friendships break up because they become emotionally exhausting. And yet what we learn from this story is that getting rid of Joseph never made his brother's lives better. Instead of working through their issues with Joseph, these men had to live with the guilt and shame of what they did all of their lives. And that should be a great lesson for us.

> **Genesis 37:29-33 Now Reuben returned to the pit, and behold, Joseph was not in the pit; so he tore his garments. He returned to his brothers and said, "The boy is not there; as for me, where am I to go?" So they took Joseph's tunic, and slaughtered a male goat and dipped the tunic in the blood; and they sent the varicolored tunic and brought it to their father and said, "We found this; please examine it to see whether it is your son's tunic or not." Then he examined it and said, "It is my son's tunic. A wild beast has devoured him; Joseph has surely been torn to pieces!"**

The boys figured they would deceive their father and once all his grief was gone, the brothers would be rid of their problem: Joseph. Their plan was to dip Joseph's coat into goat blood and lie to their father that Joseph had been killed by a wild animal. The problem with sin is that lies have to cover lies and there are always consequences.

> **Proverbs 6:16-19 There are six things which the Lord hates, yes, seven which are an abomination to Him: haughty eyes, a lying tongue, and hands that shed innocent blood, a heart that devises wicked plans, feet that run rapidly to evil, a false witness who utters lies, and one who spreads strife among brothers.**

These verses in Proverbs depict exactly what Joseph's brothers did and tells us precisely what God hates: lying, shedding innocent blood, devising wicked plans, running to evil, uttering lies and spreading strife. What they did in the heat of anger and frustration would cost them peace for most of their days, along with hurting their father deeply.

> **Genesis 37:34 So Jacob tore his clothes, and put sackcloth on his loins and mourned for his son many days. Then all his sons and all his daughters arose to comfort him, but he refused to be comforted. And he said, "Surely I will go down to Sheol in mourning for my son." So his father wept for him.**

Sin has far-reaching affects. It not only hurts the people involved but has an effect on those around you. If you are caught stealing at work, your family will have no financial means of support. If you gossip about someone, it destroys the reputation of the people involved. If you have too much to drink and get behind the wheel of a car and kill someone, you could spend time in prison.

We tell our children there are two paths in life. One is the path of wisdom – making choices today that will influence their future in a positive manner. The other is the path of a fool who makes bad choices without thinking of the future consequences. Joseph's brothers made a foolish decision based on harmful emotions and this story reminds us how devastating that can be. We have to learn to think past today and look to what the future will hold for us before we make rash and irreversible decisions.

Joseph's brothers' sin shattered the heart of their father and Joseph's younger brother Benjamin. Not only that but the brothers would have to live with what they had done all their lives. And for Joseph, his life completely changed.

Genesis 37:36 Meanwhile, the Midianites sold him in Egypt to Potiphar, Pharaoh's officer, the captain of the bodyguard.

In an instant, Joseph's life was turned upside-down. One moment he was happy at home and the next he was on his way to a foreign country as a slave. That is how fast life changes and we need to be prepared for the difficult days that come into our lives. Joseph, could have been rebellious and bitter. He could have sat around each day plotting revenge on his family. But he doesn't ever seem to do this. Somehow, he knew God was right in the middle of the frightening circumstances that came into his life.

That will always be the choice we are faced with. We can rebel against something that disrupts our life or we can add God into the equation. One will make our situation more difficult while the other can bring peace. As a Christian, God wants us to trust Him and yet it is the challenging times in our lives that give us opportunities to rely on Him. We will never know the faithfulness of God until we are put through trials that force us to depend on Him alone.

What would be your response to these scenarios?

You are fired from your job for no apparent reason…
You find out you have cancer at a very young age…
Your spouse leaves you for someone else…
The school you applied for did not accept you…
The person you are dating broke up with you for no good reason…
You lost your home and must move somewhere else…
The child you love so much is now in a rehab for drug addiction…

Your pregnancy test came back negative once again…
Someone you love was devastated by heartache…
You did not get the job you had applied for…
Someone gossiped about you and tried to ruin your reputation…
Your business failed and you had to close up shop…
Someone close to you betrayed you…

The problem is we live in a world that is constantly changing and yet somehow we want to feel in control of it all. When we realize we can't control the things that happen around us is the point when we can begin to start the "peace process." The beginning of peace is the moment we recognize that God alone is in control. When we insert Him into all the problems above we come out with a different equation and a different answer.

If you are fired from a job, you can be assured God is moving you to a different place for your own good. Maybe you will have a greater ministry and more people will come to Christ. Maybe your attitude alone will draw others to Him.

If you find out you have cancer, you can be certain God will use you in a mighty way. People need to hear about Jesus and sometimes that means even in a hospital waiting room.

If your spouse leaves, you will witness God's provision as you learn how to trust Him. You will grow as you learn how to forgive. You will be at peace knowing God has a purpose and a plan that for the moment is unseen.

If you are not accepted in the school of your choice, you can know God has plans for you somewhere else. If your child ends up in a drug rehab, recognize God has a purpose which could include a ministry to others going through similar situations.

If you cannot get pregnant, you will recognize God's timing is always perfect and He has a reason for your inability to conceive. Maybe adopting is a route He wants you to take.

If someone gossips and tries to ruin your reputation, you can be assured that God will vindicate you in His perfect timing. Nothing that anyone ever says can thwart God's purpose in your life.

If your business fails, it may seem like a failure for the moment but in the long run, God has plans beyond what you can see.

We learned this in our own lives a few years ago. For most of our married life we have owned our own businesses. At the beginning of our marriage, it never occurred to us to invite God into the business realm of our lives. For some reason we thought it was up to us to bring work in and we assumed that all the money we made was because we were just smart business owners.

Years went by and we decided to sell one of our businesses. Once that was done we were convinced we were financially set for life. We invested in land and invested in the stock market. We put money into other business ventures and during this time we were able to travel to beautiful places and purchase what we wanted.

And then in one year's time – everything changed. The stock market crashed, our real estate properties became worth pennies on the dollar and all the money we had saved had to be poured into our new business that employed four of our children. Suddenly the life we knew was gone. The money was gone, the vacations were gone, and the lifestyle was gone. Lisa came to me one day and said, "We have $262.00 left in our bank account and we have no way to pay our bills or payroll for next week."

That is why the life of Joseph is so dear to our hearts because we know what it is like when life changes. For you, it might be something completely different than a financial change. It could be a devastating personal heartache. It might be a husband or wife that walked out of your marriage or a bad report from the doctor. It could be the death of a loved one or an addiction that is destroying your life.

But change is a part of life and the reality is that we usually don't embrace change if it does not benefit us. We like it when things run smoothly. We like routine. We like to know how much money we have in our bank account. We want to know our marriage vows mean forever. But many times life does not work out that way and it is during those times that the life of Joseph can help us see the importance of putting God into each equation in our lives.

As difficult as these past few years have been, we are convinced they have been the best years of our lives. We had to learn what it truly means to trust God. We thought we always trusted Him but with money in the bank it is easy to say that. It is easy to say we trust Him when we are healthy, the marriage is solid and the kids love God. But suddenly when we are faced with circumstances out of our control, we begin to recognize that all along He is the only One really in control.

When God is inserted into the heartaches of our lives, we begin to see life from a different angle. We see a larger perspective, an eternal purpose and a reason beyond what is in front of us. For Joseph, he made the choice to accept the changes in his life. He somehow recognized that God had not abandoned him but instead He was with him. Was Joseph still sad, frustrated and afraid? Probably. But his perspective was different when He added God to all that was happening in his life.

Joseph's choice was either to be bitter and live his life negatively or be better, knowing God had a purpose behind all He allowed to come into his life. We too have the same choice. Think of how different we would be if we added God into every equation that came our way. Imagine how we could live as we recognize God has not abandoned us down here on Earth.

> **Romans 5:3-5 And not only this, but we also exult in our tribulations, knowing that tribulation brings about perseverance; and perseverance, proven character; and proven character, hope; and hope does not disappoint, because the love of God has been poured out within our hearts through the Holy Spirit who was given to us.**

God promises He will use our tribulations in life and give us PERSEVERANCE, CHARACTER and HOPE. Without trials, we will never be challenged to grow in our faith. Without difficult situations we will never know

God can and does show up for us. Joseph was learning these things as he recognized the control of his life had been severely altered. The once prize possession of his father was now torn from his home and sold into slavery in a strange land. Everything he ever knew was stripped away from him. Then, God began to show Himself in a mighty way.

Don't fight God. Find God. Come under His sovereign hand and allow Him to take all the bad in your life and turn it to good. That doesn't happen in a day or even sometimes years. Don't be angry with God. Give all of your hurt and fears to Him. He promises to take care of you and never leave you. Take one day at a time and learn His goodness and faithfulness.

> **James 1:2–4 Consider it all joy, my brethren, when you encounter various trials, knowing that the testing of your faith produces endurance. And let endurance have its perfect result, so that you may be perfect and complete, lacking in nothing.**

When your life takes an unexpected turn…
Always add God into your equation.

Chapter 3

The "New Normal"

In a moment's time - Joseph's life had a dramatic turn of events. He must have been deeply afraid as he wondered each day where his father was. He most likely kept looking down the road expecting to see his dad coming for him. And yet, day by day, nobody showed up. We are like that too. We keep expecting our lives to go back to normal and yet in order to grow up in our faith, many times God gives us a "new" normal.

The "new" normal could mean going through life single after a divorce. It could mean being jobless or suddenly sick. Maybe your "new" normal means your last child got married or went off to college. Because life changes we will have a lifetime of new experiences. The problem becomes when we can't get over how things "used" to be. We find ourselves wishing for the past, the way things were before. We can become so focused on the past that we don't know how to embrace the "now." The "now" time is what God gives us to learn new ways to trust Him – different ways to see Him work.

Somehow during the most difficult moments in Joseph's life, God used those times to grow him up spiritually. The same would be true for us. We grow to trust God when times are tough. We mature in our faith when we have nowhere else to turn. Joseph was no different and we can learn valuable lessons from his life.

Life changes in an instant. It happened to Joseph and we can be assured things will change for us also and when they do…what will we do?

Will we fall apart?
Or will we put God into the equation?

Genesis 39:1-2 Now Joseph had been taken down to Egypt; and Potiphar, an Egyptian officer of Pharaoh, the captain of the bodyguard, bought him from the Ishmaelites, who had taken him down there. THE LORD WAS WITH JOSEPH, so he became a successful man. And he was in the house of his master, the Egyptian. (Caps ours for emphasis)

In Joseph's darkest hour the Bible tells us that **"the Lord was with Joseph."** Regardless of what dark place you are in you can be assured "the Lord is with you" also. God had a purpose for Joseph and a plan for his life. He couldn't see what that could possibly be as he was going through it, but it didn't change the fact that God was still intimately involved in his life even though it likely didn't feel like it.

The same is true for you. If you are a Christian, a follower of Jesus, you can be assured that God is still with you. He might have moved you to a different place but you can know without a doubt that God has a reason for allowing what has come into your life. Joseph went from an easy life to a difficult one overnight and yet the Bible makes it clear that God never forgot where Joseph was.

Think of Joseph's life back home with his father and brothers. He was taken care of, he was coddled and pampered and yet God knew in that environment he would never grow up and be the man God needed him to be. God needed Joseph somewhere where He could stretch his faith and teach him to trust Him. And for us, God may have to do the same. He might have to put us in situations that are out of our control and uncomfortable so we can learn to lean on the only One who is in control.

When life changes for us, we need to learn how to put God into the equation. We need to recognize that when life takes a turn; our first reaction doesn't have to be "panic." Our tendency is to become fearful and anxious and we start questioning God:

> Where are You?
> Don't You see what is happening?
> Why aren't You stopping the pain?
> Why can't You give me my old life back?

And yet, when we insert God into our circumstance, the entire equation changes for us. Now, instead of questioning God we can say things like:

- "God, I **know** You are there."
- "God, I **know** You see everything that is happening."
- "God, this is so painful but I **know** You will use my pain so people see You in me."
- "God, I loved my old life but I **know** You are moving me to a new life where You want to use me."

When we add God into our situation, our lives go from an inward focus to an upward focus. Instead of looking at how discouraged we are, how pathetic our lives feel – we can now move to a more positive thought process: God is in this. It is then we have to stand on His promises:

> **Isaiah 41:17 "The afflicted and needy are seeking water, but there is none, and their tongue is parched with thirst; I, the Lord, will answer them Myself, as the God of Israel I will not forsake them."**
>
> **Psalm 94:14 "For the Lord will not abandon His people, nor will He forsake His inheritance".**
>
> **1 Samuel 12:22 "For the Lord will not abandon His people on account of His great name, because the Lord has been pleased to make you a people for Himself."**
>
> **Psalm 28:7 "The Lord is my strength and my shield; my heart trusts in Him, and I am helped; therefore my heart exults, and with my song I shall thank Him."**
>
> **Psalm 22:5 "To You they cried out and were delivered; in You they trusted and were not disappointed."**

God promises when we trust Him that He will never forsake us or abandon us. He promises He will help us. But the problem begins for many people when they trust God for something and yet He does not give them what they ask for. Instead of recognizing He has a different plan, many people walk from their faith assuming God is unfaithful. Nothing could be farther from the truth.

We have some friends who love Jesus. They have served Him faithfully. Yet, one day – in an instant – their lives were forever altered. An early morning phone call telling them their son had passed away at a young age was the most devastating news a parent could ever receive.

In the dark months after, our friend said she had always felt God was faithful until that moment. They prayed for their son. They had faith to believe God would take care of him. And yet on the day he died, it was difficult to reconcile God's faithfulness with this horrible tragedy.

The good news in this story is that this couple, just like Joseph, never walked away from their faith. Were they upset with God? Probably. Was Joseph mad at God? Probably. And both of these situations would have ended differently had our friends and Joseph refused to add God into their equation. God walked through this tragedy with them just like He did for Joseph. In their darkest hours God was with them. And in your darkest hours He will be with you too.

God does not guarantee to always give us what we want although He does promise to walk with us through our troubles and that it will work out for our good. He assures us that there will be eternal good that comes out of it. Just as in the story of Joseph, he wanted to go home; but that didn't happen. He wanted to see his dad again and yet that didn't happen for many years. He hated being a servant and yet God kept him there. Why? Because God always has a purpose for where we are – ***even if it is not where we want to be.***

We have to change our perspective when what we perceive as bad news comes into our lives. We need to factor God into everything. God cares about our relationship with Him. He cares about others coming to know Him. He cares about growing us closer to Him. Sometimes the only way that will ever happen is for Him to put difficult situations in our lives so our **only** option is Him.

Chapter 4

Moving On

One great thing about Joseph is the fact that even during the difficult days in his life, he never complained to those around him. He dug in right where he was. He didn't get depressed; he didn't let any bitterness for his brothers destroy his life. And because of his attitude, those around him saw something that set him apart from most people.

Think of how we react when something happens that we don't like. Are we constantly complaining? Are we unhappy? Are we negative to those around us? Do we continually talk about our problems to anyone who will listen? What we see from the life of Joseph, as far as we can tell from Scripture, is that people never saw a negative side to him. Instead they saw a man who trusted his God and that was very appealing to those around him.

As we are writing this, a pastor who is an American citizen, born in Iran, has been sentenced to eight years in the worst prison in Iran for his faith in Jesus. He has been beaten and tortured and yet through it all he has been a shining example to his guards and inmates. His heart is for Muslim people to come to know Jesus and God is using him in this horrendous situation to accomplish this. His wife commented on her Facebook page that as difficult as this has been on her and her two young children, it is worth it for those inside and outside the prison who have come to faith in Jesus. At one point the prison wanted to move her husband because so many men inside the prison were coming to Christ.

This man is like a modern day Joseph because we see him taking a very unpleasant situation and allowing God to use him in the midst. And yet we pray for God to get him released. We want him to be back in the comfort of his home in the United States. We would rather God open the doors of prison and get him back to his wife and children. And praying for that is not wrong. But what we do see is that as a follower of Jesus, this man has given his life to Him to do what He deems best. He has surrendered his "wants" to God's purpose for his life. He realizes that if eight years in an Iranian prison will bring people to saving faith in Jesus for all eternity then that is what really matters.

Through it all, what we learn from this Pastor and from Joseph is that when we accept where we are, what happens to those around us is they see something unusual: peace in us. Peace that can only come from serving God no matter what is thrown at us. Whether it is being jobless, sick or stuck in an Iranian prison – think about the impact our attitude has on those around us.

Consider what our purpose is as a Christian. We are to love God and share Him with those around us. But many times the people that need to hear about Jesus are in places we would rather not go such as Iranian prisons, hospital waiting rooms and unemployment lines, bars, divorce courts, retirement homes and homeless shelters. When we can begin to put God in every devastating circumstance that comes our way then we can serve Him wherever He places us. He is our reason for living and when He is at the center of our lives then wherever He puts us, we can be assured He has not forgotten us.

We see this in the life of Joseph as his master, Potiphar, recognized that God was with him. Everything in Potiphar's home was being blessed because Joseph was there and because of that, Joseph was put in charge of overseeing all that Potiphar owned.

> **Genesis 39:3-6 Now his master saw that the Lord was with him and how the Lord caused all that he did to prosper in his hand. So Joseph found favor in his sight and became his personal servant; and he made him overseer over his house, and all that he owned he put in his charge. It came about that from the time he made him overseer in his house and over all that he owned, the Lord blessed the Egyptian's house on account of Joseph; thus the Lord's blessing was upon all that he owned, in the house and in the field. So he left everything he owned in Joseph's charge; and with him there he did not concern himself with anything except the food which he ate. Now Joseph was handsome in form and appearance.**

For Joseph, life was changing. He recognized his father was not coming for him and he most likely accepted the fact he was never going back to his family. For Joseph, he decided it was time to move on and accept where God had put him.

For many of us, that is what we need to do. That could play out in any one of these scenarios:

I had money to do what I wanted all my life and now because of the economic situation I have not been able to do what I am used to doing. ***It's time to move on and enjoy where I am…***

I was married most of my life and yet my spouse walked out the door and I have to learn to do things on my own. ***It's time to move on and enjoy where I am…***

I raised my children to be a part of my life but they moved away and I am left alone. ***It's time to move on and enjoy where I am…***

I had a job I planned to retire from and I was just let go because the company downsized. ***It's time to move on and enjoy where I am…***

There are so many things I planned on doing in my life and I just found out I have a terminal illness. ***It's time to move on and enjoy where I am…***

My best friend betrayed me. ***It's time to move on and enjoy where I am…***

My employee started his own business in competition with me. ***It's time to move on and enjoy where I am…***

We need to take our cue from Joseph and realize that God is still working in our life regardless of the past. He has a plan and even the most devastating events that happen to us can be used by Him to get us where He wants us. In order for God to get Joseph to the place where He needed him, life as he knew it had to change.

And because of that, Joseph learned he had to move on, forget the past and enjoy where God had placed him. He learned that his life was filled with chapters, and the life he knew living with his fathers and brothers were gone. But God would do something new.

The great part about Joseph is that we never see him angry about his circumstances. He probably had his moments of confusion and doubt and yet from what the Bible tells us he has a great handle on the character of God. He worked for Potiphar with the greatest integrity and honor. He worked diligently. He refused to have an attitude that he was above being a servant. He didn't seem to complain. He made the best of the place God had taken him to.

As a Christian, that is what God wants from us. Because we are His children, we must learn to trust Him with all the events that come into our lives, and along with that, have a good attitude. He needs us to face new situations with joy and peace knowing all along He has never left our side. God was moving Joseph on to a new chapter in his life and yet leaving the familiar is so difficult.

> We remember the past.
> We remember what life used to be like.
> We long for the way it was before.
> We are shocked that life has taken a different path.
> We just want our old life back.

Joseph had to feel that same pain over and over as he recalled what his brothers did to him. He must have spent many nights in tears wondering how God could have allowed this to happen. He was young, he was in a foreign land, he lost his beloved father and he had to come to grips with the fact that life changes. Life is unfair sometimes.

We lose loved ones,
We lose jobs,
We lose important relationships,
We lose financial security…

And yet those are the times we are forced to get our eyes off ourselves and on to God. Those are the times we need to look past the hurt and the pain and decide in our hearts that God has not abandoned us; He is just moving us to a different place. For Joseph, his "different place" was away from his family, where God could grow him up to know Him better. We don't grow up when life is easy – we grow up when times are difficult and Joseph was the perfect example of this.

When we lost our money we realized that God wanted to grow us up. He couldn't teach us what it meant to rely on Him when we relied on our bank account. He wanted to show us He would take care of all our needs. He wanted to provide for us financially in miraculous ways so we would know it was Him who takes responsibility for us as His children. And for all the hardship in the last couple years, we can honestly say that we know Him better.

But if we are being honest then we have to say this also: there are days we miss the old life too. We just got back from a vacation on the beach that someone graciously paid for and we miss being able to pay for dinners out and stay for a month. We miss the carefree days of not worrying how we will pay the bills when get back home. Those are the times when we would really like our old life back.

And yet what we are learning is how to be content with the place God has us. As much as we would like to live the lifestyle we used to, we see that the difficult times were when we grew closer to Him. And that is most likely how Joseph felt. He probably had fond memories of what life was like back home with dad and baby brother Benjamin, but at some point he had to move on. We have to get to a point where we settle in where God has us and allow Him to have complete control over our entire life; relationships, finances and health.

Continuing on with Joseph, once he got settled into his new surroundings and God was blessing his job and Potiphar's household, a new situation arose in his young life in the form of temptation.

> **Genesis 39:7 It came about after these events that his master's wife looked with desire at Joseph, and she said, "Lie with me."**

Potiphar's wife decided she liked Joseph and offered herself to him in the form of a sexual affair. He was most likely flattered at the thought but because he knew God, he had purposed in his heart to do the right thing. He loved his job and he respected his master and regardless of the temptation he refused to succumb to her advances.

> **Genesis 39:8-10 But he refused and said to his master's wife, "Behold, with me here, my master does not concern himself with anything in the house, and he has put all that he owns in my charge. "There is no one greater in this house than I, and he has withheld nothing from me except you, because you are his wife. How then could I do this great evil and sin**

> **against God?" As she spoke to Joseph day after day, he did not listen to her to lie beside her or be with her.**

Joseph never took the easy way out. He refused her advances because of his loyalty to Potiphar. He knew his master had placed his undying trust in him and because of that; he would never do anything to destroy that relationship. But, even more than that, Joseph refused to sin against God. Somehow, despite his horrible circumstances, he never wavered from his complete trust in Him. Regardless if things were going well or badly, Joseph continued to serve God, making Him the most important, vital part of his life. Even temptation would not come between him and His relationship with God because he was a man of character and integrity.

Joseph made a great decision to add God into the temptations in his life. He knew that Joseph plus temptation could equal tragedy and yet when he added God into the equation, it allowed for his escape. So often when our lives take an unexpected turn, we blame God, but we must remember: we always have a choice. We can continue trusting Him or we can succumb to the temptations in our lives and the equation will always end up with a different answer.

Many times we rationalize sin because we feel that when we have been hurt or abandoned, we deserve some sort of comfort. Maybe it could be in the form of an illicit affair, drugs or alcohol. For Joseph, it was the offer of sex. At a young age, far from home where nobody would know, he still had a choice to make. But Joseph added God into this equation. He did what he knew to be right – he ran.

Genesis 39:11-20 Now it happened one day that he went into the house to do his work, and none of the men of the household was there inside. She caught him by his garment, saying, "Lie with me!" And he left his garment in her hand and fled, and went outside. When she saw that he had left his garment in her hand and had fled outside, she called to the men of her household and said to them, "See, he has brought in a Hebrew to us to make sport of us; he came in to me to lie with me, and I screamed. "When he heard that I raised my voice and screamed, he left his garment beside me and fled and went outside." So she left his garment beside her until his master came home. Then she spoke to him with these words, "The Hebrew slave, whom you brought to us, came in to me to make sport of me; and as I raised my voice and screamed, he left his garment beside me and fled outside." Now when his master heard the words of his wife, which she spoke to him, saying, "This is what your slave did to me," his anger burned. So Joseph's master took him and put him into the jail, the place where the king's prisoners were confined; and he was there in the jail.

Sometimes when we do the right thing it can still cause problems. If Joseph had slept with Potiphar's wife the outcome would have been devastating. Instead he did the right thing and he was falsely accused and yet the outcome was still devastating! He was put in jail.

Maybe you got fired from your job because you refused to lie for your boss. Maybe your spouse left you because you refused to watch porn. Maybe your life is in turmoil because you made the right choices. If so – you are in good company with Joseph. Just because we make good, moral decisions it doesn't always mean things will turn out for the good at that moment. But we do know they will in the long run. God will always honor doing the right things in life.

The problem is we can only see what is happening for the moment. We can't imagine that being falsely accused or fired from a job could possibly be God's best for us and yet when we look at the life of Joseph, we see God was in it all along. He was using the difficult times in Joseph's life to get him to where he was supposed to be. We need to remind ourselves that God is in the midst working behind the scenes. **Deuteronomy 29:29** says: **"The secret things belong to the Lord our God, but the things revealed belong to us and to our sons forever, that we may observe all the words of this law."**

If you have been damaged by hurtful people or tragedies in your life, remember that you must put God in the equation. You plus your pain could equal depression and anxiety but you plus pain plus God equals the knowledge that He is in control. With that knowledge you will be able to continue on in the midst of your struggles, knowing that just like Joseph, God has not abandoned you.

Chapter 5

Attitudes

Joseph was now in prison for doing the right thing and once again he had a choice: be angry and depressed, or recognize God was with him and have a good attitude. All of us have the same choice. When life changes and our world is turned upside down, we can smile and live with a joyful attitude knowing God is up to something good or we can be miserable. Joseph is a great example of someone who did not let his circumstances rule his life. He took what came to him and made the best of all the obstacles put in front of him.

> **Genesis 39:21-23 But the Lord was with Joseph and extended kindness to him, and gave him favor in the sight of the chief jailer. The chief jailer committed to Joseph's charge all the prisoners who were in the jail; so that whatever was done there, he was responsible for it. The chief jailer did not supervise anything under Joseph's charge because the Lord was with him; and whatever he did, the Lord made to prosper.**

No matter what difficulties come into our lives, we can choose what attitude we want others to see. Evidently, Joseph had an uplifting outlook even in a prison after being falsely accused. How do we get there? How can we smile and be joyful when our world seems to be falling apart? How can we trust that God will come through for us? Here are three thoughts that might help.

1. We have to know God. We have to spend time reading our Bible so we can see His character. The more we know Him the easier it will be to trust Him. Think about the people closest to you. We assume you are close because you spent time with them. The same would be true with God – we will never know Him if we don't spend the time reading His Word.

   When we were going through our financial difficulties the one place we were compelled to go to was our Bible. We would camp out on verses that showed God's miraculous provisions to His people. And as we would read these verses over and over – they weren't just words on a page. They became promises to us from God - which gave us hope.

Here are a few of the verses:

Psalm 22:4–5 (AMP) Our fathers trusted in You; they trusted (leaned on, relied on You, and were confident) and You delivered them. They cried to You and were delivered; they trusted in, leaned on, and confidently relied on You, and were not ashamed or confounded or disappointed.

The Amplified Bible was key to helping us understand what the word "trust" really meant. We needed to remember that we weren't the first people to ever have problems! We needed to see that other people in times past who were hurting also cried out to Him, leaned on Him and were confident that He was listening. Their stories gave us hope that He would deliver us also.

We spent a lot of time in 2 Chronicles 20 as we read about Jehoshaphat, a King in the Old Testament. He heard a report that a great army was coming against him and it struck fear in his heart. For us it probably won't be an army but it could be the inability to pay a bill, a meeting with the school's principal or an interview that determines if you get the job you need.

> **2 Chronicles 20:2 Then some came and reported to Jehoshaphat, saying, "A great multitude is coming against you from beyond the sea, out of Aram and behold, they are in Hazazon-tamar (that is Engedi)."**
>
> **3 Jehoshaphat was afraid and turned his attention to seek the LORD, and proclaimed a fast throughout all Judah.**

There would be weeks in our business where we had no way to pay our bills and during those days it was easy to become fearful. When we took the time to open our Bible we would read that men like Jehoshaphat were also fearful. Knowing that became a source of comfort for us. Seeing how he handled his fear encouraged us to continue to trust that God could do anything knowing He was still in control.

Reading the Bible shows us how others responded to fear. For Jehoshaphat, instead of going into depression, running away or drinking too much, he put his efforts into seeking God. He spent the time looking upward for help and not inward to self-pity. When we read His Word and recognize that everything in the Bible is meant to teach us something about who God is and how He wants us to live our lives – then we can live life how God intended.

> **4 So Judah gathered together to seek help from the LORD; they even came from all the cities of Judah to seek the LORD.**
>
> **5 Then Jehoshaphat stood in the assembly of Judah and Jerusalem, in the house of the LORD before the new court,**
>
> **6 and he said, "O LORD, the God of our fathers, are You not God in the heavens? And are You not ruler over all the kingdoms of the nations? Power and might are in Your hand so that no one can stand against You.**
>
> **7 "Did You not, O our God, drive out the inhabitants of this land before Your people Israel and give it to the descendants of Abraham Your friend forever?**

The first thing Jehoshaphat did was tell God who he knew Him to be: Creator of the heavens and ruler over nations, powerful and mighty. As Jehoshaphat did that, it became a reminder to him how authoritative his God was in whatever fearful situation was thrown at him. And that is a great lesson for us to learn. When we are put in situations where fear begins to reign, our first response should be remembering who God is.

14 Then in the midst of the assembly the Spirit of the LORD came upon Jahaziel the son of Zechariah, the son of Benaiah, the son of Jeiel, the son of Mattaniah, the Levite of the sons of Asaph;

15 and he said, "Listen, all Judah and the inhabitants of Jerusalem and King Jehoshaphat: thus says the LORD to you, 'Do not fear or be dismayed because of this great multitude, for the battle is not yours but God's.

17 'You need not fight in this battle; station yourselves, stand and see the salvation of the LORD on your behalf, O Judah and Jerusalem.' Do not fear or be dismayed; tomorrow go out to face them, for the LORD is with you."

And this is how we get to know God. We read His Word about people just like us who struggled with the same fears as we do. We read about how big and powerful our God is. What we learn over and over is that the battle is the Lord's. Our lack of finances, lack of jobs, and lack of health becomes His battle to take care of. We do what we can and leave the rest to Him. When we do this, we begin to look at our problems in light of God's plan for our lives, instead of what we expect out of our lives.

Psalm 28:7 "The Lord is my strength and my shield; my heart trusts in Him, and I am helped; therefore my heart exults, and with my song I shall thank Him."

Psalm 31:4 "You will pull me out of the net which they have secretly laid for me, for You are my strength."

2. We have to continually tell ourselves the truth. We need to recite verses. We need to remind ourselves that God has not abandoned us. But remember, we can't talk to ourselves about something we don't know. Our son is getting ready to take the test for his driving permit and there is a manual he will have to study to pass the test which will allow him to drive. If he doesn't study, he won't know how to answer the questions.

   The same is true for us. When we have questions about our lives and why things are happening, if we haven't studied His manual – the Bible – we will not have the answers. When we don't have answers, we are confused and fumble around in the dark. But if we know the answers the test becomes simple.

Psalm 105:4 Seek the Lord and His strength; seek His face continually.

This verse is a reminder of the importance of seeking Him all the time – not just when something bad happens. If we seek Him continually then when something comes into our lives unexpectedly, we are prepared. We need to renew our mind daily which means we have to replace the negative thoughts with positive thoughts. We need to take a pessimistic situation and turn it positive by putting God into the equation. We need to continually put in our minds the things of God.

Romans 12:2 And do not be conformed to this world, but be transformed by the renewing of your mind, so that you may prove what the will of God is, that which is good and acceptable and perfect.

3. We must allow God to fight our battles for us knowing He will avenge those who have hurt us.

Deuteronomy 32:35 'Vengeance is Mine, and retribution, in due time their foot will slip; for the day of their calamity is near, and the impending things are hastening upon them.'

Romans 12:19 Never take your own revenge, beloved, but leave room for the wrath of God, for it is written, "Vengeance is Mine, I will repay," says the Lord.

When we are hurt by people, our first instinct is to get back at the person who hurt us. Yet our attitude can be altered by knowing this: God will fight our battles for us because He is the great Vindicator. Joseph must have known that God would take care of his brothers who sold him to slave traders, and Potipher's wife who lied about him. Surely Joseph was angry by what they had done and yet his life was not wrought with bitterness and hatred. We have to learn how to do the same: trust our enemies to God or let them destroy us on the inside.

At the beginning of this book, we told you about a person hurting someone we loved. It was difficult to watch and yet the only thing we knew how to do was to fight back with the Words of God. We had to go to His promises daily and stand on them. Reading through the

Psalms one day, it was clear that King David had enemies and people who hurt him also. Reading how David's heart was broken somehow gave us the comfort we needed. If someone has hurt you, stand on the promises that God will take care of your situation.

Psalm 35 A Psalm of David.
Contend, O Lord, with those who contend with me;
Fight against those who fight against me.
Take hold of buckler and shield and rise up for my help.
Draw also the spear and the battle-axe to meet those who pursue me;
Say to my soul, "I am your salvation."
Let those be ashamed and dishonored who seek my life;
Let those be turned back and humiliated who devise evil against me.
Let them be like chaff before the wind, with the angel of the Lord driving them on.
Let their way be dark and slippery, with the angel of the Lord pursuing them.
For without cause they hid their net for me; without cause they dug a pit for my soul.
Let destruction come upon him unawares, and let the net which he hid catch himself;
Into that very destruction let him fall.
And my soul shall rejoice in the Lord; it shall exult in His salvation.
All my bones will say, "Lord, who is like You,
Who delivers the afflicted from him who is too strong for him,
and the afflicted and the needy from him who robs him?"

Malicious witnesses rise up; they ask me of things that I do not know.
They repay me evil for good, to the bereavement of my soul.
But as for me, when they were sick, my clothing was sackcloth;
I humbled my soul with fasting, and my prayer kept returning to my bosom.
I went about as though it were my friend or brother;
I bowed down mourning, as one who sorrows for a mother.
But at my stumbling they rejoiced and gathered themselves together;
The smiters whom I did not know gathered together against me,
They slandered me without ceasing.
Like godless jesters at a feast, they gnashed at me with their teeth.
Lord, how long will You look on? Rescue my soul from their ravages,
My only life from the lions.
I will give You thanks in the great congregation;
I will praise You among a mighty throng.
Do not let those who are wrongfully my enemies rejoice over me;
Nor let those who hate me without cause wink maliciously.
For they do not speak peace,
but they devise deceitful words against those who are quiet in the land.
They opened their mouth wide against me; they said, "Aha, aha, our eyes have seen it!"
You have seen it, O Lord, do not keep silent; O Lord, do not be far from me.

Stir up Yourself, and awake to my right And to my cause, my God and my Lord.
Judge me, O Lord my God, according to Your righteousness,
And do not let them rejoice over me.
Do not let them say in their heart, "Aha, our desire!"
Do not let them say, "We have swallowed him up!"
Let those be ashamed and humiliated altogether who rejoice at my distress;
Let those be clothed with shame and dishonor who magnify themselves over me.
Let them shout for joy and rejoice, who favor my vindication;
and let them say continually, "The Lord be magnified,
Who delights in the prosperity of His servant."
And my tongue shall declare Your righteousness and Your praise all day long.

In a sense, it seems wrong to pray this Psalm. Let their path be slippery? Let destruction come upon them? That doesn't sound like the words of Jesus which say we should pray for our enemies. And yet David had to learn to be honest with God and allow God to take vengeance on those who hurt him. Otherwise, the hurt and anger would build up in David and he would want to retaliate.

This Psalm was written many years after Joseph had died and yet we see a pattern that in a fallen world – we too, will most likely be hurt at one time or another. What we do with that hurt is up to us. How we respond to those who hurt us will depend on how well we know God and His retribution. We serve a God who sees our hearts and if we have humble and broken and contrite hearts – He will surely take care of our enemies for us.

Our job is to pray that we will have the ability to treat our enemy in love and have the ability to pray for them.

> **Matthew 5:44-45** says:**"But I say to you, love your enemies and pray for those who persecute you, so that you may be sons of your Father who is in heaven; for He causes His sun to rise on the evil and the good, and sends rain on the righteous and the unrighteous.**

Why? Why would God want me to pray for those who have hurt me? Because He knows how harmful it is to keep anger inside of us. He knows how it will affect us physically and also mentally. Joseph could have fallen into depression, refused to go on with his life and treated everyone around him poorly because of the wrong that had been done to him. Instead, Joseph trusted God to handle his enemies for him. He woke up each morning with a smile on his face and a song in his heart because he knew his life was under the sovereign control of God. We can do the same.

Can we be honest here? That takes effort on our part. That takes time in His Word. That takes prayer. That takes trusting the Holy Spirit to change us from the inside. But that means one thing: we have to make a conscious effort to keep God in front of us at all times.

One Friday night we decided to go to a football game. Walking out of the gate that night we came face to face with the person who was causing so much grief to someone we love. And guess what we did? Hugged?

Blessed? Smiled at? No, we did everything we could to make sure this person knew the word "shunned." We walked by, looking the other way, making sure our disgust was shown by our actions. Amazing for people who write Christian books about love.

But what we learned is how that anger and bitterness was eating us up and how we could not allow that to take root in our lives. We had to learn to stop it before it destroyed us. And we did that by continually acknowledging a few things:

1. God could have stopped this entire hurtful situation from occurring. We serve a big God who could have stopped the hurt this person caused, and yet knowing that He didn't helped us push through our heartache. Now we are armed with the understanding that if He did not stop it, then He wants to use it.

Isaiah 45:5-7 "I am the Lord, and there is no other; besides Me there is no God. I will gird you, though you have not known Me; that men may know from the rising to the setting of the sun that there is no one besides Me. I am the Lord, and there is no other, the One forming light and creating darkness, causing well-being and creating calamity; I am the Lord who does all these."

2. We must live in the supernatural. We live in a natural world where we trust what we see in front of us. Being a Christian means that as we learn about God, we start living more in the supernatural than the natural. This means that,

just like Joseph, we will be able to focus on what God is doing by faith, rather than what we see in front of us. Joseph saw in the natural world that his brothers sold him into slavery to get rid of him. But in the supernatural realm Joseph trusted that God was moving him to where he was supposed to be. The same would be true with Potiphar's wife. Joseph was most likely heartbroken that his integrity was compromised and yet he somehow knew that in the supernatural, God was moving him once again.

Romans 8:28-31 And we know that God causes all things to work together for good to those who love God, to those who are called according to His purpose. For those whom He foreknew, He also predestined to become conformed to the image of His Son, so that He would be the firstborn among many brethren; and these whom He predestined, He also called; and these whom He called, He also justified; and these whom He justified, He also glorified. What then shall we say to these things? If God is for us, who is against us?

3. God has a purpose beyond what we can see. For us, we can only see what is happening today. We sometimes forget there is a future and God is using our today to shape the rest of our lives. When we can constantly remind ourselves of that fact, then we can relax and trust that God is allowing this time in our life for something beyond what we can see at the moment.

Proverbs 16:4 The Lord has made everything

for its own purpose, even the wicked for the day of evil.

Isaiah 46:10-11 Declaring the end from the beginning, and from ancient times things which have not been done, saying, 'My purpose will be established, and I will accomplish all My good pleasure'; calling a bird of prey from the east, the man of My purpose from a far country. Truly I have spoken; truly I will bring it to pass. I have planned it, surely I will do it.

Sometimes we have a small view of God and therefore we tend to forget He can do anything He wants to. When we are going through difficult times in our lives - when everything seems hopeless, the economy is going under, and the morals of our nation are failing, we tend to forget that we serve a mighty God who is still in control.

In the Bible there is a story of a man named Job who learned this very lesson. He loved God and served Him faithfully and yet in one day his entire world came crashing down.

Job 1:13-21 Now on the day when his sons and his daughters were eating and drinking wine in their oldest brother's house, a messenger came to Job and said, "The oxen were plowing and the donkeys feeding beside them, and the Sabeans attacked and took them. They also slew the servants with the edge of the sword, and I alone have escaped to tell you." While he was still speaking, another also came and said, "The fire of God fell from heaven and burned up the sheep and the servants and

> **consumed them, and I alone have escaped to tell you." While he was still speaking, another also came and said, "The Chaldeans formed three bands and made a raid on the camels and took them and slew the servants with the edge of the sword, and I alone have escaped to tell you." While he was still speaking, another also came and said, "Your sons and your daughters were eating and drinking wine in their oldest brother's house, and behold, a great wind came from across the wilderness and struck the four corners of the house, and it fell on the young people and they died, and I alone have escaped to tell you." Then Job arose and tore his robe and shaved his head, and he fell to the ground and worshiped. He said, "Naked I came from my mother's womb, And naked I shall return there. The Lord gave and the Lord has taken away. Blessed be the name of the Lord."**

In one day Job lost his children, his servants, and his livestock which would constitute being a really, really bad day. We would be hard pressed to think of anything worse and yet along with the tragedy of losing everyone and everything important to him, Job ended up with boils all over his body. In the natural realm, what Job was going through made no sense. Yet thousands of years later we have a picture of God that we would never have if He had not allowed this tragedy in Job's life.

When things happen out of our control and we start to question God, Job 38 through 41 reminds us how big our God is. What we see is God reminding Job of who He really is. As we are going through our own personal struggles in our lives, we need to be reminded that

God can do anything He wants to and if He withholds something from us, there is a reason. Job learned this as God reiterated to him who He really is.

Job 38:1-3 Then the Lord answered Job out of the whirlwind and said, "Who is this that darkens counsel by words without knowledge? "Now gird up your loins like a man, and I will ask you, and you instruct Me!

Job 38:4-7 "Where were you when I laid the foundation of the earth? Tell Me, if you have understanding, Who set its measurements? Since you know. Or who stretched the line on it? "On what were its bases sunk? Or who laid its cornerstone, when the morning stars sang together and all the sons of God shouted for joy?

Job 38:8-11 "Or who enclosed the sea with doors when, bursting forth, it went out from the womb; when I made a cloud its garment and thick darkness its swaddling band, and I placed boundaries on it and set a bolt and doors, and I said, 'Thus far you shall come, but no farther; and here shall your proud waves stop'?

Job 38:12-13 "Have you ever in your life commanded the morning, and caused the dawn to know its place, that it might take hold of the ends of the earth, and the wicked be shaken out of it?

Job 38:16-17 "Have you entered into the springs of the sea or walked in the recesses of the deep? "Have the gates of death been revealed to you, or have you seen the gates of deep darkness?

Job 38:18-21"Have you understood the expanse of the earth? Tell Me, if you know all this. "Where is the way to the dwelling of light? And darkness, where is its place, that you may take it to its territory and that you may discern the paths to its home? "You know, for you were born then, and the number of your days is great!

Job 38:22-23 "Have you entered the storehouses of the snow, or have you seen the storehouses of the hail, which I have reserved for the time of distress, for the day of war and battle?

Job 38:31-33 "Can you bind the chains of the Pleiades, or loose the cords of Orion? "Can you lead forth a constellation in its season, and guide the Bear with her satellites? "Do you know the ordinances of the heavens, or fix their rule over the earth?

Job 39:27-30 "Is it at your command that the eagle mounts up and makes his nest on high? "On the cliff he dwells and lodges, upon the rocky crag, an inaccessible place. "From there he spies out food; his eyes see it from afar. "His young ones also suck up blood; and where the slain are, there is he."

When God is through questioning Job, the only response Job can give is this:

> **Job 42:1-6 Then Job answered the Lord and said, "I know that You can do all things, and that no purpose of Yours can be thwarted. 'Who is this that hides counsel without knowledge?' "Therefore I have declared that which I did not understand, things too wonderful for me, which I did not know." 'Hear, now, and I will speak; I will ask You, and You instruct me.' "I have heard of You by the hearing of the ear; but now my eye sees You; therefore I retract, and I repent in dust and ashes."**

What changed Job's attitude was the knowledge of who God is. God CAN do all things. NO purpose of His can be thwarted. He is the God who created eagles, stars and ocean waves. He is the God who created light and darkness, snow and lightning. We serve a mighty God who can change our situations in a moment's notice. We need a high view of God in order to take us through the challenging events in our lives, and we need to trust He can change a person, heal a sickness, and restore a relationship. But, we recognize that His involvement is on His timing.

Joseph seemed to understand this about God. He somehow knew that God was big enough to deal with his brothers and his destroyed reputation which enabled him to have a good attitude. That is where we need to get to in our lives. The more we know God, the easier it is to walk through this life trusting Him to use our difficult moments to show others how we live supernaturally. The natural is where most people live, but in the supernatural we can live by faith believing His purposes are far greater than what we can imagine. Joseph allowed for God to take vengeance on those who hurt him and seeing Joseph do this gives us hope that we too can do the same.

Chapter 6

God's Timing

Joseph is now in prison but God has given him favor in the sight of the chief jailer. Joseph has been put in charge of all the prisoners and God begins moving people in and out of his life who eventually will be the avenue for his release. Unfortunately for Joseph, the time spent in prison will be longer than he ever imagined and yet God is using the time in prison and the people he will encounter to change the course of history.

In prison, Joseph meets a cupbearer and a baker who used to be employed by the King. Somehow they both had enraged the Pharaoh and landed in jail where Joseph was put in charge of taking care of them.

> **Genesis 40:1-6 Then it came about after these things, the cupbearer and the baker for the king of Egypt offended their lord, the king of Egypt. Pharaoh was furious with his two officials, the chief cupbearer and the chief baker. So he put them in confinement in the house of the captain of the bodyguard, in the jail, the same place where Joseph was imprisoned. The captain of the bodyguard put Joseph in charge of them, and he took care of them; and they were in confinement for some time. Then the cupbearer and the baker for the**

king of Egypt, who were confined in jail, both had a dream the same night, each man with his own dream and each dream with its own interpretation. When Joseph came to them in the morning and observed them, behold, they were dejected.

Many people wonder how God speaks to us today and one way is through His written Word, the Bible. He also speaks to us through the Holy Spirit who indwells each of us if we are His children. But back in the days of Joseph, the Bible was not available so God spoke through prophets, dreams and visions.

As we read earlier, one of the reasons Joseph's brothers hated him was because God had given him two dreams that alluded to the fact he would rule over his brothers. We wonder if that is what kept Joseph going through the difficult years knowing it was God who had spoken to him. Maybe his dreams were confirmation of God's hand in his life and that is why he was able to endure the hardship that came his way.

For us, we have the Bible that is filled with promises and affirmations regarding God's hand in all we do. He promises if we are His children, He will guide us, love us, provide for us and never leave us. He promises to work all things out for good even if our circumstances look bleak. We can stand on God's promises just like Joseph must have done in his life. We will be able to handle anything that comes our way when we know that, just like Joseph, God is with us through it all.

As Joseph languishes in prison, what we see is that he knows the cupbearer and the baker on a deeper level than just guard and prisoner. He was acquainted with them well enough to know they were deeply troubled one particular day. Joseph cared about people regardless of where he was. He was in prison for something he did not do. He was hated by his brothers and sold into slavery. His past was one of heartache and despair and yet he chose to be joyful and pleasant and to care for those around him.

Joseph cared enough for others to know when someone was distraught and instead of being inward focused, his choice was to be outward focused. Something was bothering the baker and the cupbearer and instead of walking on by, he chose to ask them about their day and what was bringing them such distress.

> **Genesis 40:6-8 When Joseph came to them in the morning and observed them, behold, they were dejected. He asked Pharaoh's officials who were with him in confinement in his master's house, "Why are your faces so sad today?" Then they said to him, "We have had a dream and there is no one to interpret it." Then Joseph said to them, "Do not interpretations belong to God? Tell it to me, please."**

Something in Joseph's past probably rang in his mind as he remembered his dreams that nobody else understood. He was determined to take this seriously since when he was a boy he was laughed and scoffed at.

> **Genesis 40:9-13 So the chief cupbearer told his dream to Joseph, and said to him, "In my dream, behold, there was a vine in front of me; and on the vine were three branches. And as**

it was budding, its blossoms came out, and its clusters produced ripe grapes. "Now Pharaoh's cup was in my hand; so I took the grapes and squeezed them into Pharaoh's cup, and I put the cup into Pharaoh's hand." Then Joseph said to him, "This is the interpretation of it: the three branches are three days; within three more days Pharaoh will lift up your head and restore you to your office; and you will put Pharaoh's cup into his hand according to your former custom when you were his cupbearer.

Good news for the cupbearer. God had given Joseph the ability to discern the meaning of his dream and he told the cupbearer that in three days he would have his job back. Joseph was probably getting excited knowing God had just given him the interpretation of this dream and he most likely became hopeful that this event would help further his own release from jail.

Genesis 40:14-15 "Only keep me in mind when it goes well with you, and please do me a kindness by mentioning me to Pharaoh and get me out of this house. "For I was in fact kidnapped from the land of the Hebrews, and even here I have done nothing that they should have put me into the dungeon."

Joseph offers a plea for his life and for the first time he seems to defend himself. He explains he was kidnapped from his homeland and innocent of the crimes he was accused of and all he asked of the cupbearer was to let the king know. Imagine how Joseph must have felt: finally a ray of hope! Harpers Bible Dictionary defines hope like this: "the expectation of a favorable future under God's direction." There is something in all of us that needs to feel that God will eventually bring something good into our lives from all the bad.

Sometimes we lose hope because our circumstances become overwhelming. We have a friend who is the most positive person we know and yet one day everything seemed to hit her at once. Her daughter couldn't find a job and she was in pain all the time from an injury that was forcing her to have surgery. Changes to her job were adding stress and it was 118 degrees out in Phoenix in the summer! Even so, the one thing she knew she couldn't lose was hope that God would change her situation for the better.

All through the Psalms we see King David struggle with the despair of life but despite that he put his hope in God. We all have days, like our friend where it seems like things will not get better. Our example is David who is honest with God and places his hope where it needs to be: in Him. Looking at the life of David, he had bad days and bad weeks which many times led to bad years. But what he never did was give up hope that God was intimately a part of his life in the good times and the bad.

> **Psalm 43:5 "Why are you in despair, O my soul? And why are you disturbed within me? Hope in God, for I shall again praise Him, the help of my countenance and my God."**

> **Psalm 31:24 "Be strong and let your heart take courage, all you who hope in the LORD."**

> **Psalm 39:7 "And now, Lord, for what do I wait? My hope is in You."**

> Solomon reminds us in **Ecclesiastes 7:14 "In the day of prosperity be happy, but in the day of adversity consider— God has made the one as well as the other so that man will not discover anything that will be after him."**

Don't lose hope. Don't lose the belief that God will come through for you in His time and in His way. Hang on to that just like Joseph did as he sat in prison interpreting the butler's and baker's dreams hoping that at last, someone would hear his story and vouch for his integrity.

> **Genesis 40:16-19 When the chief baker saw that he had interpreted favorably, he said to Joseph, "I also saw in my dream, and behold, there were three baskets of white bread on my head; and in the top basket there were some of all sorts of baked food for Pharaoh, and the birds were eating them out of the basket on my head." Then Joseph answered and said, "This is its interpretation: the three baskets are three days; within three more days Pharaoh will lift up your head from you and will hang you on a tree, and the birds will eat your flesh off you."**

When the baker saw that Joseph had interpreted the cupbearer's dream in a favorable manner, he decided to see what his own future would hold. Unfortunately for him, he only had three days to live and Pharaoh would put him to death. Not so good news for the chief baker.

> **Genesis 40:20-22 Thus it came about on the third day, which was Pharaoh's birthday, that he made a feast for all his servants; and he lifted up the head of the chief cupbearer and**

> **the head of the chief baker among his servants. He restored the chief cupbearer to his office, and he put the cup into Pharaoh's hand; but he hanged the chief baker, just as Joseph had interpreted to them.**

Just as Joseph had told both the baker and the cupbearer, one was given his job back and the other was put to death. Joseph must have felt some comfort knowing the cupbearer would resume his position near the King and now he had a chance to be pardoned. Of course the cupbearer would remember Joseph. Of course he would be so profoundly thankful for Joseph and the comfort he had been given in jail that he would remember to let Pharaoh know of Joseph's plight.

But, unfortunately for Joseph, that never happened. Joseph will learn once again; God's timing is not always our timing.

> **Genesis 40:23 Yet the chief cupbearer did not remember Joseph, but forgot him.**

The cupbearer forgot him? How does that happen? If someone pulls you from a burning building, you don't forget them! If someone pays your rent because they know you are struggling, you don't forget them! If someone recommends you for a job and you get it, you don't forget them! So what is the problem?

God's perfect timing is the problem.

We can imagine Joseph's excitement as he packed his bags awaiting the news of his release. But in God's economy – until it is His perfect timing – it won't happen. We have a man trying to raise money for our business and he is amazed that he hasn't been able to get anyone to commit. It doesn't shock us because what we see is God's hand holding people back. We don't know why but our hope is in Him to provide what we need when we need it. Is it frustrating? Yes. Are we confused about what God is doing? Yes. But when we read the story of Joseph and how God kept him two more years in prison and then we see the outcome - that gives us hope and comfort.

What we see in God's Word is that God needed Joseph to help save Egypt from a severe famine, which is why He was not ready to release Joseph yet. All the pieces were not put into place. Sadly, one more disappointment was added to Joseph's life and he would be in prison for two more years.

God's timing can be so frustrating. We yearn to get pregnant… now. We need the business deal to go through…now. We desire to have a better marriage… now. The problem is that we waste so much of our lives questioning God. We wonder where He is. We doubt His love for us when our lives take a turn for the worst. We squander each 24 hour day given to us, confused and dissatisfied with our lot in life. What we need is a good dose of Joseph.

Joseph was not able to see his future. He only saw each day as the same. Wake up, help the prisoners, do the same tasks, and go to bed in order to wake up and do it all over again. Yet in hindsight we are able to see what he was never able to see in the natural: the hand of God leading and guiding.

We see God moving in his brother's hearts allowing the hatred to fester. ***God needed Joseph in Egypt***. We see God moving in Potiphar's life to hire Joseph knowing full well that Potiphar's wife would play the role of seductress. ***God needed Joseph in prison***. We see the Pharaoh's anger toward the baker and the cupbearer as part of God's overall plan. ***God needed Joseph to interpret their dreams***. God allowed the cupbearer to be restored for God's perfect timing. ***God needed Joseph to see the King***.

If only we could look at life this way.

Our son Jesse went to Wheaton College in Illinois. His football career reminded us of a modern day "waiting on God" story that we wanted to include in this chapter. Here is Jesse's story:

> *My football career started in junior high, I can remember asking my mom if I could play and with a concerned sigh and my dad's approval I joined the 8th grade team at Phoenix Christian High. I did not realize at the time that this was the start of a long and tough journey. I was a kid just excited to play the game I had come to know and love.*
>
> *The 8th grade season of football was a crucial year because it implanted the love of the greatest game on my heart. God used this season in my life to give me direction that would pave the way through High School and College; a way that would forever change my outlook on life.*
>
> *It was freshman year at Phoenix Christian High School and football season had started. Up north at*

football camp the reality began to set in. This was no longer junior high, this was high school football. Everyone was bigger, faster and hit harder. Little did I know, this was nothing compared to college football.

High school football was difficult; I was the type of athlete that had to work harder than a lot of the other guys with natural ability. I did have natural talent but not enough to make it on ability alone. I had to train hard and work out with a speed coach to get my 40 time down. I didn't see the varsity field as a starter until my senior year. The coaches had me at Tight End and Linebacker my senior year. Wanting to play both ways, the coaching staff made an executive decision to have as many one way players as possible. My heart was set at Linebacker but the coaching staff started me at Tight End.

My senior year was one of the greatest years when it came to football. The team was close and we made some pretty amazing goals. 13-0 undefeated State Champs was simply the only option; enough so that we all wrote 13-0 on our brand new Nike cleats so we could see it every time we looked down. It was a long road to state but we made it and won with a perfect record. In fact, we had the best defense in state history with only 27 points scored on us all year! I ended the season making All State honorable mention Tight End; a great way to end high school.

As high school was coming to a close, I will never forget browsing the websites to see which college I wanted to attend. I searched long and hard until God had me stumble upon Wheaton College located just outside Chicago. As I read the website and the coaches' profiles I realized this was the place for me, not knowing at the time that a family friend was currently playing football there. I spoke with my friend and handed him my highlight tape to give to the coaches when he returned from break.

After Christmas break I received a call from Coach Sandberg saying they reviewed the tape and would like me to come out for a visit. He also asked if there were any other players that would be interested in Wheaton. I told him about my good buddy Geoff and that Wheaton would benefit greatly from a player like him.

So Geoff and I were on a plane headed out to Chicago to check out the school and the football program. We both loved the coaches and the school and made a decision to apply. We went through the rigorous application process that Wheaton has and both were waiting to hear the results.

I will never forget the phone call I received from Coach Sandberg. It was a late school night and coach said, "Jesse, I am sorry to tell you that you were not accepted." He went on to say, "Geoff has been accepted and approved to play in our football program. If you really want to be a part of the Wheaton team, you will need to attend a community college for a year and re-apply next year." After the conversation, I hung up the phone and immediately went into my parent's room. They were sound asleep and I woke them up. I said, "I just got a call from Sandberg and I was not accepted." I remember my mom said, "Oh no…Jesse I am so sorry." I told them both right then and there that God has a plan and it's all going to be ok.

Spring break came and we headed to Hawaii with the family to visit my brother Sean at YWAM. My buddy Geoff came with the family on this vacation. I will never forget sitting on the beach looking out at the ocean when my dad received a phone call. With excitement in his voice he said, "Are you serious Phil, wow that is really cool." He got off the phone and said Wheaton had accepted my application outside of the football program and that I will be attending with Geoff in the fall! Geoff and I jumped up from the hot sand and screamed. We were so pumped! As best friends, we were Chicago bound football players in just a few short months. God knew exactly what He was doing! Not on my timing, not on my parents timing…on HIS timing!

August 2004: trailer loaded, bags packed and Chicago bound. This was the start of a new chapter in my life. I would say one of the most important chapters when it came to God shaping me into the man He wanted me to be.

I will never forget the practice freshman year when I had no clue what I was doing on Special Teams and coach asked me to hold the football and took me out of the drill. This was a foreshadowing of what the next three years would entail. Keep in mind; I came into the program as basically a walk on. My acceptance into Wheaton was outside the football program. I had to prove myself on this team and the next three years were an uphill battle.

Wheaton College has a great football program, My teammate Andy Studebaker got drafted to the NFL in the 6th round to the Philadelphia Eagles and now plays Linebacker for the Chiefs. Wheaton is NCAA Division III top 25 pretty much every year. Coach Swider is an amazing Head Coach. It is bar none one of the best D3 programs in the country. These were the caliber of athletes I played with and was competing with for a starting position.

I played outside Linebacker and my best friend Mike McKinney played the same position. He was by far a better athlete than me. We used to call him Mini-Mouse because he was short and quick. I will never forget senior year watching Mike go down pre-season. It was an obvious ACL tear but we didn't know how bad it really was. The MRI and X-ray results showed not only a complete blow out but also cartilage damage. This meant a special kind of surgery and a lot longer recovery time. Mike was out his senior season, for good. This meant I was in.

I will never forget starting on that football field. All this hard work these last 3 years had finally paid off. All the morning workouts at 6am in the off season puking in a trash can, all the long hours lifting weights, all the blood, sweat and tears was finally paying off. Coach Swider used to always say, "Disciplined are the people who can sacrifice and work with no immediate return."

It was October 13th, 2007, we were playing Augustana College at home under the lights. In the 4th quarter, "Augustana methodically moved the ball downfield, getting the ball to the Thunder seven-yard line with 47-seconds left in the game thanks to a fourth-down conversion on a 10-yard pass from Ryan McGinnis to Matt Downing. With four downs to reach the end zone Augustana spiked the ball to stop the clock on first down and two incompletions gave the guests one play remaining to reach the end zone. Thunder linebacker Jesse Laizure stormed through the Vikings' offensive line and sacked McGinnis to give the Thunder the ball and the victory." (Wheaton Website: http://athletics.wheaton.edu/news/2007/10/13/FB-AUGIE.aspx) Watch at YouTube.com "Jesse Laizure's game ending sack against Augustana. (http://www.youtube.com/watch?v=2fjICIkNsQ0)

There I was - the walk on at Wheaton, a backup player, on a highly ranked football team making the game winning, walk off sack against our rival team, at home, under the lights, with my entire family watching! The lesson God taught me since the moment I stepped on my first football field in 8th Grade was that you have to persevere and keep fighting despite the circumstances. You never know when you will get your chance to shine. For me, it took seven long years of discipline and hard work to get just one moment of glory in time. In the end, the glory was God's. He was the One who guided my steps those seven years. He was the One who allowed me to go through hard times of doubt. He was the One who taught me all the life lessons, and in the end He was the one who received all the glory.

When Jesse first went to Wheaton he had to stay in Illinois for Thanksgiving. When we called to wish him a happy Thanksgiving he told us it was snowing and they were shoveling snow off the football field. His dad was proud and his mom was sad he wasn't home where it was warm and comfortable. But in order to get where God wants us, most of the time it isn't comfortable.

Jesse learned what Joseph learned which was: don't quit – have a good attitude – do your best – work your hardest and wait on God's perfect timing. If he had taken his mom's attitude of comfort, turkey and mashed potatoes, he would have missed the greatest moment of his football career. Good thing he listened to his dad.

As Winston Churchill said: "Never, never, never give up."

Principles we can learn from Joseph are things like this:

> Heartaches bring new opportunities.
>
> Disappointments lead to deeper faith.
>
> Lack of finances lead to trusting God on a higher level.
>
> Sickness brings a deeper dependence on God.

Think what could happen if we looked at life in this manner. What if we saw God in everything – the good, the bad, the heartache, and the disappointments? What if we knew, just like Joseph, that God was with us? What if we knew, beyond a shadow of a doubt, that God was using everything to get us to a new place where we trust Him more, love Him more, and serve Him more?

What if we never looked at our problems as problems, but instead we saw them as God ordained opportunities?

What if we saw each sorrow as a platform to show others about God?

What if we recognized that a loss of a job, a relationship or a possession was not a bad thing but rather a God ordained event to get us to a better place?

What if – we added God into the equation of every circumstance that comes our way?

Me + Problem + God = God's perfect timing.

Chapter 7

Finally

Genesis 41:1-7 Now it happened at the end of two full years that Pharaoh had a dream, and behold, he was standing by the Nile. And lo, from the Nile there came up seven cows, sleek and fat; and they grazed in the marsh grass. Then behold, seven other cows came up after them from the Nile, ugly and gaunt, and they stood by the other cows on the bank of the Nile. The ugly and gaunt cows ate up the seven sleek and fat cows. Then Pharaoh awoke. He fell asleep and dreamed a second time; and behold, seven ears of grain came up on a single stalk, plump and good. Then behold, seven ears, thin and scorched by the east wind, sprouted up after them. The thin ears swallowed up the seven plump and full ears. Then Pharaoh awoke, and behold, it was a dream.

Finally the years of waiting are over for Joseph. Two years later, after the cupbearer is released, Joseph finally gets his big break. As we will see, God uses his past experiences, his past relationships and his gift of interpreting dreams to come together at the perfect time in order for God to use him for this specific purpose. For Joseph, his old life seemed like a lifetime ago. His father was a distant memory. His homeland was quickly forgotten. Joseph would now embark on a new life that would be "exceedingly, abundantly beyond all he could ask or think." (Ephesians 3:20, our paraphrase).

> **Genesis 41:8-14 Now in the morning his spirit was troubled, so he sent and called for all the magicians of Egypt, and all its wise men. And Pharaoh told them his dreams, but there was no one who could interpret them to Pharaoh. Then the chief cupbearer spoke to Pharaoh, saying, "I would make mention today of my own offenses. "Pharaoh was furious with his servants, and he put me in confinement in the house of the captain of the bodyguard, both me and the chief baker. "We had a dream on the same night, he and I; each of us dreamed according to the interpretation of his own dream. "Now a Hebrew youth was with us there, a servant of the captain of the bodyguard, and we related them to him, and he interpreted our dreams for us. To each one he interpreted according to his own dream. "And just as he interpreted for us, so it happened; he restored me in my office, but he hanged him." Then Pharaoh sent and called for Joseph, and they hurriedly brought him out of the dungeon; and when he had shaved himself and changed his clothes, he came to Pharaoh.**

Finally, the cupbearer remembered Joseph! Isn't that just like God? We assume we will get a certain job but after being turned down, we get something better a year later. We think this relationship will last a lifetime only to see after the breakup there is someone even more suitable for us. Waiting and wondering. Questioning and confusion. And then God shows up in the most unlikely way imaginable. Joseph is called by the Pharaoh himself, thanks to all the people in his past that made that moment possible. His jealous, hateful brothers. His married boss's wife who wanted to sleep with him. The cupbearer who completely forgot he existed.

When all hope seems gone…that is when God comes through.

Remember that if your days are dark at this moment, God always seems late. He always seems to have forgotten us. And yet, just like Joseph, God is right on time. Not our time but God's time. He has a plan for our lives. He has a purpose for our days on Earth. And we have a choice.

We can:

- Run from God when times get difficult.
- Walk away from our faith because He didn't come through when we think He should have.
- Become angry with God assuming He doesn't care.
- Stop going to church and reading our Bibles thinking this "God thing" doesn't really work.

Or we can:

- Wait on God knowing His timing is perfect.
- Continue walking in faith regardless if our prayers seem unanswered.
- Trust that God knows what He is doing.
- Look at every circumstance as God ordained, moving us to a new place.

Suddenly, Joseph has a meeting with the Pharaoh and with a new pair of clothes and a newly shaved face, he meets with him one on one.

> **Genesis 41:15-16 Pharaoh said to Joseph, "I have had a dream, but no one can interpret it; and I have heard it said about you, that when you hear a dream you can interpret it." Joseph then answered Pharaoh, saying, "It is not in me; God will give Pharaoh a favorable answer."**

For all the troubles in Joseph's life, he never turned his back on God. He never took credit for having the ability to interpret dreams. And now, when standing in front of the most powerful man in Egypt, Joseph gave God all the credit and honor that was due. Joseph knew God alone would give him the capability to interpret Pharaoh's dream.

We can understand what God saw in Joseph and why He took him on the journey He did. Joseph was loyal to those he served. He lived his life with integrity. He persevered under trial. He was kind and compassionate to others. He trusted God regardless of his circumstances. He honored God with the gifts he was given. Just like David was deemed a "man after God's own heart," Joseph surely was the man who "refused to walk away from his faith."

And when it came time to promote Joseph, he was ready. He was now God's man for the job who weathered the storms and heartaches of life. He was prepared because he knew that approximately 15 years earlier, God had spoken to him in a dream and gave him hope for the future. He couldn't understand it at the time and yet he never gave up on his dream.

If you have a dream and desire for something you feel God has laid on your heart, don't give up. Maybe it is a ministry, a specific job, a degree or a diploma. Maybe it is the desire to be married or have children or start a business. If you feel God is leading you to something and yet you are still waiting; remember Joseph. Be patient. Know what you are going through is a training ground and God is your teacher. Learn what He is imparting in your life. And then, when the dream is realized, give Him all the praise and honor and glory due Him for making it possible.

We have a friend who needed a job. She was hired on as a seasonal employee at a large corporation with the hopes of being kept on permanently when the holidays were over. Everyone loved her. She was a hard worker. There was not even a question in everyone's minds that she would not be one of the ten hired on for a permanent position.

But she wasn't. The manager for no apparent reason did not like her. Out of fifteen people, ten stayed on and she was let go. Just like Joseph she was confused and sad for the moment. As the days wore on the other people who had been let go were re-hired; everyone but her. And so, she had a choice. She could take it personally and go into depression. She could feel bitter or angry with God and the manager. And yet, she didn't.

She trusted that God moved on the manager's heart not to hire her. She knew the Bible said in **Proverbs 21:1** that **"The king's heart is like channels of water in the hand of the LORD; He turns it wherever He wishes."** She added God into her equation and recognized His hand in turning the manager away from hiring her. She didn't have to take it personally when God was involved in this situation. It gave her great opportunities to trust in God alone.

The time spent not working allowed her to start a Women's Bible Study group. By working full time, she would not have been able to add this to her life. Once her Tuesday study was set up, she got a call from the company and they wanted to rehire her; not only for part time but a full time position with Tuesday's off! God was in it all along, just like He was with Joseph and like He is with each of us. He always has a purpose for the "no's" and the "detours." His timing is always perfect.

Adding God into the equation makes us recognize His sovereign control over our lives. Me plus my dream does not equal much unless God is involved. Me plus my dream plus God assures me that my dream is in His hands. He is molding me and shaping me until He feels I am ready for the challenge and then I can walk through life seeing His purpose for me. Wait – don't run away.

Just like Joseph – it is all in due time; ***it is all in His time***.

Chapter 8

New Seasons

Life is filled with seasons. The problem most of us share is this overwhelming feeling that when things are good, we never want it to end. But the Bible gives us a different picture of life. It isn't always pleasant. There are good times and bad. There are happy times and sad. Joseph experienced them all.

For us, we need to remember that things change. The economy changes, the children grow up and businesses are bought and sold. We buy new homes. We lose our health. The Bible is clear that our lives do not remain stagnant. We got a call from our son this morning telling us his mother in law was taken to the hospital because of a possible stroke. We told him to start expecting this in his life since we are getting older and life changes. He said he wished we could freeze time which we politely reminded him that if we froze time his two year old daughter would freeze in this age. Enough said…!

Ecclesiastes 3 tells us what to expect out of life:

> **Ecclesiastes 3:1-11**
>
> **There is an appointed time for everything.**
> **And there is a time for every event under heaven**
> **A time to give birth and a time to die; a time to plant and a time to uproot what is planted.**

> **A time to kill and a time to heal; a time to tear down and a time to build up.**
> **A time to weep and a time to laugh; a time to mourn and a time to dance.**
> **A time to throw stones and a time to gather stones;**
> **A time to embrace and a time to shun embracing.**
> **A time to search and a time to give up as lost; a time to keep and a time to throw away.**
> **A time to tear apart and a time to sew together; a time to be silent and a time to speak.**
> **A time to love and a time to hate; a time for war and a time for peace.**
> **What profit is there to the worker from that in which he toils?**
> **I have seen the task which God has given the sons of men with which to occupy themselves.**
> **He has made everything appropriate in its time.**

Joseph spent his life learning these principles. When life changed for Joseph, he understood God was present wherever he was being led. We have that choice also. We can either recognize God is moving us from season to season – or we can live a frustrated, joyless, angry existence. The way Joseph handled his seasons should give us hope that we too have the same capacity.

Even through all the seasons Joseph had been through, he was about to enter one that even he would not believe possible. From prison to palace. From guard over prisoners to the second in command to Pharaoh. A new season with a new job – and all ordained by God who had been grooming him and moving him to the place where he was needed.

Genesis 41:17-30 So Pharaoh spoke to Joseph, "In my dream, behold, I was standing on the bank of the Nile; and behold, seven cows, fat and sleek came up out of the Nile, and they grazed in the marsh grass. "Lo, seven other cows came up after them, poor and very ugly and gaunt, such as I had never seen for ugliness in all the land of Egypt; and the lean and ugly cows ate up the first seven fat cows. "Yet when they had devoured them, it could not be detected that they had devoured them, for they were just as ugly as before. Then I awoke. "I saw also in my dream, and behold, seven ears, full and good, came up on a single stalk; and lo, seven ears, withered, thin, and scorched by the east wind, sprouted up after them; and the thin ears swallowed the seven good ears. Then I told it to the magicians, but there was no one who could explain it to me." Now Joseph said to Pharaoh, "Pharaoh's dreams are one and the same; God has told to Pharaoh what He is about to do. "The seven good cows are seven years; and the seven good ears are seven years; the dreams are one and the same. "The seven lean and ugly cows that came up after them are seven years, and the seven thin ears scorched by the east wind will be seven years of famine. "It is as I have spoken to Pharaoh: God has shown to Pharaoh what He is about to do. "Behold, seven years of great abundance are coming in all the land of Egypt; and after them seven years of famine will come, and all the abundance will be forgotten in the land of Egypt, and the famine will ravage the land.

Joseph was able to interpret Pharaoh's dream explaining that Egypt was in for a devastating famine; but before that would happen there would be seven years of abundance. Pharaoh was being fore-warned by God what was about to happen, and Joseph was right there at the right time completely ordained by God.

Genesis 41:31-46 "So the abundance will be unknown in the land because of that subsequent famine; for it will be very severe. "Now as for the repeating of the dream to Pharaoh twice, it means that the matter is determined by God, and God will quickly bring it about. "Now let Pharaoh look for a man discerning and wise, and set him over the land of Egypt. "Let Pharaoh take action to appoint overseers in charge of the land, and let him exact a fifth of the produce of the land of Egypt in the seven years of abundance. "Then let them gather all the food of these good years that are coming, and store up the grain for food in the cities under Pharaoh's authority, and let them guard it. "Let the food become as a reserve for the land for the seven years of famine which will occur in the land of Egypt, so that the land will not perish during the famine." Now the proposal seemed good to Pharaoh and to all his servants. Then Pharaoh said to his servants, "Can we find a man like this, in whom is a divine spirit?" So Pharaoh said to Joseph, "Since God has informed you of all this, there is no one so discerning and wise as you are. "You shall be over my house, and according to your command all my people shall do homage; only in the throne I will be

> **greater than you." Pharaoh said to Joseph, "See, I have set you over all the land of Egypt." Then Pharaoh took off his signet ring from his hand and put it on Joseph's hand, and clothed him in garments of fine linen and put the gold necklace around his neck. He had him ride in his second chariot; and they proclaimed before him, "Bow the knee!" And he set him over all the land of Egypt. Moreover, Pharaoh said to Joseph, "Though I am Pharaoh, yet without your permission no one shall raise his hand or foot in all the land of Egypt." Then Pharaoh named Joseph Zaphenath-paneah; and he gave him Asenath, the daughter of Potiphera priest of On, as his wife. And Joseph went forth over the land of Egypt. Now Joseph was thirty years old when he stood before Pharaoh, king of Egypt. And Joseph went out from the presence of Pharaoh and went through all the land of Egypt.**

In one day, Joseph's life changed forever. In one day he went from prisoner overseeing prisoners to Pharaoh's right hand man. A signet ring, new clothes, jewelry, a chariot and a new wife were quite a bit different than a dungeon, prison clothes, lonely and an unshaven face. Joseph went from a season of suffering to a season of success. That is how fast our lives can change.

Think about a day which consists of a 24 hour period. In that small amount of time God can change your situation just like he did for Joseph. Your pregnancy test can be positive. You can meet the person you will marry. You can be hired for a job. You can get news the cancer is in remission. You can get a phone call from your wayward child. All in a day. All in a moment. That is the God we serve.

In a 24 hour period Jesus was crucified on a cross that brought devastation and confusion to those who followed Him. And then, in a different 24 hour period, on the third day, He was resurrected and changed the course of history. In one day, death was defeated and life was made possible. One day. That is all God needs to change our circumstances.

The best part about this is Joseph wasn't even expecting this day to be any different from the rest. He had his normal routine and was shocked when he heard Pharaoh wanted to see him. Up to that point, Joseph could only trust God daily for his needs.

Are you wondering how you will pay your bills?

Are you concerned about the salvation of a loved one?

Are you fearful you won't get a job?

Are you worried about what tomorrow may bring?

If so, we need to remember Joseph. God met his needs every day he was in prison. He was with him. He was directing those around him. And when God was ready to move Joseph from one season to the next, God's timing was perfect. Joseph did not see it at the time, just like we may not, and yet we have the privilege of looking back on his life and seeing God's hand as he moved him from place to place. We need to recognize that what God did for Joseph, he does for us also.

> **Philippians 4:12-13 I know how to get along with humble means, and I also know how to live in prosperity; in any and every circumstance I have learned the secret of being filled and going hungry, both of having abundance and suffering need. I can do all things through Him who strengthens me.**
> **Philippians 4:19 And my God will supply all your needs according to His riches in glory in Christ Jesus.**

Just like He did for Joseph, God promises to supply all our needs. Joseph learned that having prosperity or poverty meant little to him as long as he never lost his faith in God. We can lose possessions and lose relationships but somehow knowing God has allowed those things is what will get us through. We have learned that God's timing is always perfect and in one day – one short 24 hour period – God can change it all. This is the story of hope. And that is what can happen when we add God back into our equation regarding the seasons in our lives.

Chapter 9

Forgetting the Past

Life is filled with hurtful situations and yet God calls us to forget the past. **Philippians 3:13** says: **Brethren, I do not regard myself as having laid hold of it yet; but one thing I do: forgetting what lies behind and reaching forward to what lies ahead**. We need to remember that our past is what has brought us to our future. Just like Joseph – the devastation his brothers brought him could have scarred him for life and yet Joseph refused to allow that to happen. He added God into the equation and the answer came out different. Joseph plus hurt equals bitterness but Joseph plus hurt plus God equals peace.

> **Genesis 41:46-49 Now Joseph was thirty years old when he stood before Pharaoh, king of Egypt. And Joseph went out from the presence of Pharaoh and went through all the land of Egypt. During the seven years of plenty the land brought forth abundantly. So he gathered all the food of these seven years which occurred in the land of Egypt and placed the food in the cities; he placed in every city the food from its own surrounding fields. Thus Joseph stored up grain in great abundance like the sand of the sea, until he stopped measuring it, for it was beyond measure.**

The first seven years Joseph worked diligently to store as much food as possible in preparation for the famine. Instead of working hard he could have taken a trip back home. He could have tried to retaliate for what his brothers did to him. He could have been angry and sulked and complained about how unfair life was but he did not do that. Rather, he trusted that God had a plan and leaving his homeland approximately 15 years earlier was all part of it.

Maybe for you it was a painful divorce you cannot get over. Perhaps someone stole from you, gossiped about you or lied to you. Possibly someone did not meet your expectations and you have never forgiven them. In life, without adding God into your problem, the answer will never have its proper sum. Look at the life of Joseph and change your perspective. God allowed his brothers to do what they did in order to get Joseph in the position he needed to be in. That is what God is doing with you. Look at your past circumstances with eternal glasses and see if you can see a purpose beyond the pain.

For Joseph, along with his new job came a new family which included a new wife and two new sons. How blessed Joseph must have felt to move on to a new chapter in his life. **Genesis 41:51-52** explains how even naming his children meant he trusted God's involvement. **"Joseph named the firstborn Manasseh, "For," he said, "God has made me forget all my trouble and all my father's household." He named the second Ephraim, "For," he said, "God has made me fruitful in the land of my affliction."**

Look at your life today. Maybe like Joseph you have felt suffering and hardship brought on by someone else. But

Joseph's story should give you hope that you can live a fruitful life even with a devastating past. Why? Because regardless of Joseph's difficult days, the Bible makes it clear that **"The Lord was with Joseph."** The problems in Joseph's life made him the man he became. That is why we can forgive others – because we recognize God can use those complicated times to mold us into the people He needs us to be.

Joseph has left a legacy by his life and that is what God wants from us. He wants to show others that as followers of Christ, we have the power through the Holy Spirit to love and forgive those who hurt us. He wants us as His children to rise above the bitter, resentful feelings and show a watching world that we are different. We look at the world through the eyes of God. We have added Him into the equation and the answer is one of comfort and tranquility.

How do we do that? We recognize God's hand in the entirety of our lives. From the day we were born – God was there.

> **Psalm 39:4-5 says "LORD, make me to know my end and what is the extent of my days; let me know how transient I am. Behold, You have made my days as handbreadths, and my lifetime as nothing in Your sight; surely every man at his best is a mere breath."**
>
> **Psalm 139:13-14 For You formed my inward parts; You wove me in my mother's womb. I will give thanks to You, for I am fearfully and wonderfully made; wonderful are Your works, and my soul knows it very well.**

Psalm 139:16 Your eyes have seen my unformed substance; and in Your book were all written the days that were ordained for me, when as yet there was not one of them.

We can forget the past and forgive those who hurt us because nothing in our lives happened by accident. Just like Joseph, the hurt and pain were allowed by God to get him to the place God needed him. Look at your life with the same lenses. The painful divorce is allowing God to move you to a better place. The loss of your job is permitting you to move to a new and better job. Yes it feels devastating, but knowing God is in it, changes how we can react.

Here is the truth to tell ourselves when we want to recall the past hurt:

Life is short.
God wove me in my mother's womb.
My birth was not an accident therefore my life has a purpose.
God is intricately involved in all the days of my life.
God has ordained my life even before I was born.

When we begin to get this, it will change our lives. We do not have to be burdened by past hurts because we know that is how God has gotten us to where we are today. Just like Joseph, the pain is what allowed him to become second in command to Pharaoh and help save many people from starvation. When we insert God into the hurt, the answer will always be "there is a purpose." Move forward in your life knowing this. Forgive those who hurt you knowing they were part of God's plan to get you where you need to be. Pray for those who hurt you because God does not want you to go through life angry and unforgiving. Look at life through the eyes of God and His purpose for your life.

Ephesians 4:32 "Be kind to one another, tender-hearted, forgiving each other, just as God in Christ also has forgiven you."

Chapter 10

Sowing and Reaping

We all have people in our lives who have hurt us. Maybe it was a business relationship that was broken up over greed. Possibly it was a friendship that dissolved over hurtful words. The only way to get over these issues in our lives is to recognize that God's answer to this issue is this: we reap what we sow.

Joseph sowed honesty and integrity into his life and is now reaping the benefits of his actions. His brothers, on the other hand, have sowed deception into their lives and are now about to reap the consequences of what they had done almost twenty years before.

Once the seven years of plenty were over, the difficult days of famine were ahead.

> **Genesis 41:53-57 When the seven years of plenty which had been in the land of Egypt came to an end, and the seven years of famine began to come, just as Joseph had said, then there was famine in all the lands, but in all the land of Egypt there was bread. So when all the land of Egypt was famished, the people cried out to Pharaoh for bread; and Pharaoh said to all the Egyptians, "Go to Joseph; whatever he says to you, you shall do." When the famine**

was spread over all the face of the earth, then Joseph opened all the storehouses, and sold to the Egyptians; and the famine was severe in the land of Egypt. The people of all the earth came to Egypt to buy grain from Joseph, because the famine was severe in all the earth.

God was at work in Joseph's life all along. He gave him favor with Pharaoh, enabled him to interpret the dream warning of the famine to come, and then put him in the position to help others get food during the dark days of the food shortage. And then, God steps in and does something SO unexpected as Joseph comes face to face with his past. His brothers have come all the way from their home looking for food.

Genesis 42:1-6 Now Jacob saw that there was grain in Egypt, and Jacob said to his sons, "Why are you staring at one another?" He said, "Behold, I have heard that there is grain in Egypt; go down there and buy some for us from that place, so that we may live and not die." Then ten brothers of Joseph went down to buy grain from Egypt. But Jacob did not send Joseph's brother Benjamin with his brothers, for he said, "I am afraid that harm may befall him." So the sons of Israel came to buy grain among those who were coming, for the famine was in the land of Canaan also. Now Joseph was the ruler over the land; he was the one who sold to all the people of the land. And Joseph's brothers came and bowed down to him with their faces to the ground.

Back in Canaan where Joseph's father and brothers lived, the famine had been severe. They heard there was grain in Egypt and so Jacob, Joseph's father, sent his sons to get food for their family. Jacob sent all his boys except Benjamin, Joseph's younger brother. It is amazing to see that Jacob did not learn his lesson regarding having favorite children since Joseph's younger brother Benjamin was not allowed to go for fear of something bad happening to him. Benjamin was Joseph's full blood brother and for Jacob, their father, he was the only living link to the woman he loved who died giving birth to him; Rachel.

Imagine the scene as Joseph looked out at his brothers as they bowed down before him. What a surprise to see the men who sold him into slavery some twenty years before. They were older and most likely desperate. They were hungry and their families were in need of food. And as Joseph looked up, his stomach must have churned at the shock of who was standing in front of him.

But what must have astonished him the most was the recollection of the dream he had when he was a boy; the dream that drove his brothers to hate him and sell him into slavery.

> **Genesis 37:5-11 Then Joseph had a dream, and when he told it to his brothers, they hated him even more. He said to them, "Please listen to this dream which I have had; for behold, we were binding sheaves in the field, and lo, my sheaf rose up and also stood erect; and behold, your sheaves gathered around and bowed down to my sheaf." Then his brothers said to him, "Are you actually going to reign over us? Or**

> **are you really going to rule over us?" So they hated him even more for his dreams and for his words. Now he had still another dream, and related it to his brothers, and said, "Lo, I have had still another dream; and behold, the sun and the moon and eleven stars were bowing down to me." He related it to his father and to his brothers; and his father rebuked him and said to him, "What is this dream that you have had? Shall I and your mother and your brothers actually come to bow ourselves down before you to the ground?" His brothers were jealous of him, but his father kept the saying in mind.**

And this was the moment he had dreamt about years before. In an instant his mind had to flash back to the dream God had given him as a young boy; a dream foretelling that his family would bow down to him. What did not make sense to Joseph as a young boy suddenly came full circle. Finally…the dream God gave him as a boy was coming to fruition.

Through all the years of sadness and turmoil, it was becoming clear that this moment had been ordained from before he was born. God had a plan to save the lives of many and he would use a Hebrew boy that was hated by his step brothers to do so. The reasons for all of the frustrating years of slavery, false accusations and being forgotten in prison were rapidly becoming clear to him.

The lesson we can learn from this is that life is filled with difficult days. What we learn from the life of Joseph is that troubled days do not mean God has forgotten us. The silent times are not indications that God is not present with us. As a follower of Jesus we have to remember that the Holy Spirit lives within us so He hasn't gone anywhere – He just chooses to be quiet. And as God – that is His prerogative.

What we learn from men in the Bible like Joseph, David and Job is that they had to decide if their faith was genuine. Faith that is real trusts God has a purpose in the dark days. Faith that is sincere will push past the "why" questions and continue on believing there is a reason for what does not make sense. Faith is born and grows in the times when we cannot understand what God is doing and yet we refuse to walk away.

We live in a world where there is pain. As we are writing this we were asked to pray for a four year old diagnosed with Stage 4 Cancer. Family, friends and people they do not know are praying for a miracle. But we live in a world where there is heartache and tragedy and it is during those times that our faith is tested. Will we still love God when the verdict is in? Will we still praise Him when the divorce is final, the child never recovers or the business deal falls through?

And that is what we can learn from Joseph. Years and years later, after anxiety and fear, heartache and disappointment - God shows up and we can see in hindsight that He was in it all along. When we can add Him to each ordeal that life throws at us, we can be assured that He has never left us. Joseph has proven that to us as he is confronted by his past.

Imagine the moment he saw his family! Imagine the questions he wanted to ask! How's Benjamin? Is dad still alive? But through it all, he never made himself known as Joseph. For all they knew, the man speaking with them was a full blown Egyptian. He was dressed like one, talked like one and only an Egyptian close to Pharaoh would be in charge of all the grain in the land. Not one thing said made the brothers think they were bowing down to their long lost brother who they had sold into slavery decades earlier.

> **Genesis 42:7-11 When Joseph saw his brothers he recognized them, but he disguised himself to them and spoke to them harshly. And he said to them, "Where have you come from?" And they said, "From the land of Canaan, to buy food." But Joseph had recognized his brothers, although they did not recognize him. Joseph remembered the dreams which he had about them, and said to them, "You are spies; you have come to look at the undefended parts of our land." Then they said to him, "No, my lord, but your servants have come to buy food. "We are all sons of one man; we are honest men, your servants are not spies."**

At this point, Joseph seems harsh and uncompassionate with his brothers. Maybe the pain of his past hits him full force. Possibly his anger begins to rise. Mostly it seems he just wants the truth about his father and brother Benjamin and therefore he begins to take desperate measures to find out the legitimacy of what they are telling him.

For you, it might be seeing your ex-spouse after so many years. Possibly someone hurt you as a child and you came face to face with them at a theme park. Maybe the person who fired you which forced you into bankruptcy showed up at your church. And what you feel is just what Joseph felt – shock and emotions that you don't know how to cope with.

And what Joseph does is buy some time, which is a really good plan. Instead of striking out or saying things you will regret, get some time and space between you and the situation in order to get your emotions in balance.

> **Genesis 42:12-17 Yet he said to them, "No, but you have come to look at the undefended parts of our land!" But they said, "Your servants are twelve brothers in all, the sons of one man in the land of Canaan; and behold, the youngest is with our father today, and one is no longer alive." Joseph said to them, "It is as I said to you, you are spies; by this you will be tested: by the life of Pharaoh, you shall not go from this place unless your youngest brother comes here! "Send one of you that he may get your brother, while you remain confined, that your words may be tested, whether there is truth in you. But if not, by the life of Pharaoh, surely you are spies." So he put them all together in prison for three days.**

What Joseph does is give himself three days. He can't trust a word his brothers are telling him because he doesn't know them. The last time he saw them they conspired to kill him, so in order to confirm the truth he puts them all in jail for three days. He needs time to think. He needs time to come up with a plan to see if what they are telling him is the truth. His main concern is finding out if his father and Benjamin are truly alive.

Genesis 42:18-20 Now Joseph said to them on the third day, "Do this and live, for I fear God: if you are honest men, let one of your brothers be confined in your prison; but as for the rest of you, go, carry grain for the famine of your households, and bring your youngest brother to me, so your words may be verified, and you will not die." And they did so.

After the three days are up, Joseph decides to test them regarding their character. He offers a trade: take grain to your family while one brother is held in prison in Egypt and the others go home and bring Benjamin back to Joseph. This will prove to Joseph that his brothers are telling the truth.

As they try to determine what to do, they begin conversing about their past and what they did to Joseph. Because Joseph spoke Egyptian and he had a translator, his brothers had no idea Joseph knew the Hebrew language and understood every word that was being spoken.

Genesis 42:21-23 Then they said to one another, "Truly we are guilty concerning our brother, because we saw the distress of his soul when he pleaded with us, yet we would not listen; therefore this distress has come upon us." Reuben answered them, saying, "Did I not tell you, 'Do not sin against the boy'; and you would not listen? Now comes the reckoning for his blood." They did not know, however, that Joseph understood, for there was an interpreter between them.

The guilt of what they had done in their past had never left them. They remembered how Joseph pleaded for his life and they refused to listen. They recognized their past was coming back to haunt them. They are reaping what they sowed.

The Bible is clear in **Galatians 6:7-9** that the attitudes and actions we sow will reap in the future that same kind of harvest.

"Do not be deceived, God is not mocked; for whatever a man sows, this he will also reap. For the one who sows to his own flesh will from the flesh reap corruption, but the one who sows to the Spirit will from the Spirit reap eternal life. Let us not lose heart in doing good, for in due time we will reap if we do not grow weary."

For Joseph's brothers, they sowed envy, loathing and bitterness. They sowed the seeds of lying and deceitfulness and 20 years later they are reaping the consequences of those actions.

The same is true for us today: whatever we sow we will reap.

If you want to reap a good marriage you need to sow the seeds of love, kindness and selflessness.

If you sow seeds of bitterness, anger and selfishness you will reap a bad marriage.

If you want to reap the benefits of a good job you will sow seeds of honesty, hard work and integrity.

If you sow seeds of laziness, dishonesty and compromise you will reap the loss of your job.

Joseph's brothers had made a rash decision based on harmful emotions when they were younger and now they recognize with full force the implications of what they did. And as Joseph listened to his brothers confess to each other how they harmed him many years earlier, this was his response in verse 24:

He turned away from them and wept.

Suddenly, Joseph recognizes how the pain of what his brothers had done is still present in their lives at that moment. Was it fear they were feeling? Regret for what they had done? Or was it a painful memory that they could never, ever forget. Whatever it was, when Joseph heard them talking he turned away and wept.

This had to be a monumental moment for Joseph as he listened in on his brother's conversation. He saw them saddened by what they had done. It was that moment of truth when they recognized their sin – they spoke it out loud. "We destroyed our brother." "We refused his cries." "We are being punished for our actions so long ago." No longer did they push it under the carpet but actually spoke the words out loud.

That is the first step to repentance: recognizing what we have done as an injustice against God's commands. Then, we turn from those hurtful actions and move to make better choices.

Genesis 42:24-25 - But when he returned to them and spoke to them, he took Simeon from

> **them and bound him before their eyes. Then Joseph gave orders to fill their bags with grain and to restore every man's money in his sack, and to give them provisions for the journey. And thus it was done for them.**

Joseph could have destroyed every one of them but instead chose the path to grace. He filled their bags and gave them their money back because he needed to know if they would come back for Simeon. Would they lie to their dad? Would they say Simeon died along the way? Had they grown up and learned from their past mistakes?

We also may have to learn this lesson from Joseph in our own lives. Perhaps for you it is an abusive ex-husband wanting to come back home claiming he has changed. Possibly it is a child on drugs who says he is clean. And maybe like Joseph you will need to make sure what they say is true before you can let them back in your everyday life.

For Joseph, giving them their money back along with grain gave them the opportunity to lie to their father once again, or be truthful and come clean about Simeon in an Egyptian jail. Joseph needed to know if they would do the right thing this time. And this test is just what it would take for Joseph to know the truth.

Always remember:

Whatever we sow in our lives…
That is what we will reap.

Whatever decisions we make during the course of the day will be sowing to one of two things:

THE FLESH or THE SPIRIT

Galatians 5:16-23 But I say, walk by the Spirit, and you will not carry out the desire of the flesh. For the flesh sets its desire against the Spirit, and the Spirit against the flesh; for these are in opposition to one another, so that you may not do the things that you please. But if you are led by the Spirit, you are not under the Law. Now the deeds of the flesh are evident, which are: immorality, impurity, sensuality, idolatry, sorcery, enmities, strife, jealousy, outbursts of anger, disputes, dissensions, factions, envying, drunkenness, carousing, and things like these, of which I forewarn you, just as I have forewarned you, that those who practice such things will not inherit the kingdom of God. But the fruit of the Spirit is love, joy, peace, patience, kindness, goodness, faithfulness, gentleness, self-control; against such things there is no law.

Are you sowing…

immorality, impurity, sensuality, idolatry, sorcery, enmities, strife, jealousy, outbursts of anger, disputes, dissensions, factions, envying, drunkenness, carousing,

Or are you sowing…

love, joy, peace, patience, kindness, goodness, faithfulness, gentleness, self-control

Remember, God's equation looks like this:

You + sowing a good attitude or action = reaping blessing.

You + sowing a bad attitude or action = reaping trouble.

That is God's equation for a good life. Sometimes, sowing good happens immediately and yet many times like in Joseph's life, it takes years to see the final outcome. Our job is to live our lives making decisions based on God and His Word.

When we add God into the equation of sowing and reaping it will forever change our outlook on those who have hurt us. For Joseph, he is about to see this first hand.

Chapter 11

Restoring Relationships

A new chapter is coming into the life of Joseph and all the years of deception are about to come to an end. But first he needs to know the character of his brothers who hurt him so badly years before. Had they changed? Or were they the same lying, conniving, jealous men he knew growing up? As the brother's ride away from Egypt with Simeon in jail, they open their sacks and realize that not only do they have grain but their money has been returned. Sheer terror strikes their hearts.

> **Genesis 42:26-28 So they loaded their donkeys with their grain and departed from there. As one of them opened his sack to give his donkey fodder at the lodging place, he saw his money; and behold, it was in the mouth of his sack. Then he said to his brothers, "My money has been returned, and behold, it is even in my sack." And their hearts sank, and they turned trembling to one another, saying, "What is this that God has done to us?"**

Somehow they recognized God was in the midst of their situation. They knew what they had done in their past and the guilt of what they had done was resurfacing. They attached the fear in their lives with God's discipline but instead of lying to their father like they did twenty years before, they come clean about Egypt. They learned from their past which is great news for us. It means we too can come clean, be forgiven and move on with our future.

What this shows us is that people can change. These men were filled with hatred and jealousy. They had murderous hearts with evil intentions. They were liars and deceivers. And yet years later we see these men broken over their past and completely changed men. They don't lie to their father. They don't lie to Joseph. Everything in their lives becomes an open book because they learned the hard way what deceit will do to a person.

Over time these men changed which gives us hope that we can too. Just because you used to be an alcoholic doesn't mean you always have to be. Just because you used to be a drug addict doesn't mean that is your path for life. God's specialty is changing us from the inside out but in order for that to happen we have to recognize our sin and come clean with God and with those we hurt. Then, like Joseph's brothers, we can move on.

> **Genesis 42:29-38 When they came to their father Jacob in the land of Canaan, they told him all that had happened to them, saying, "The man, the lord of the land, spoke harshly with us, and took us for spies of the country. "But we said to him, 'We are honest men; we are not spies. 'We are twelve brothers, sons of our father; one is no longer alive, and the youngest is with our father today in the land of Canaan.' "The man, the lord of the land, said to us, 'By this I will know that you are honest men: leave one of your brothers with me and**

> **take grain for the famine of your households, and go. 'But bring your youngest brother to me that I may know that you are not spies, but honest men. I will give your brother to you, and you may trade in the land.' " Now it came about as they were emptying their sacks, that behold, every man's bundle of money was in his sack; and when they and their father saw their bundles of money, they were dismayed. Their father Jacob said to them, "You have bereaved me of my children: Joseph is no more, and Simeon is no more, and you would take Benjamin; all these things are against me." Then Reuben spoke to his father, saying, "You may put my two sons to death if I do not bring him back to you; put him in my care, and I will return him to you." But Jacob said, "My son shall not go down with you; for his brother is dead, and he alone is left. If harm should befall him on the journey you are taking, then you will bring my gray hair down to Sheol in sorrow."**

The famine was intense and yet Jacob refused to let Benjamin go. Somehow he blamed Joseph's brothers for the loss of Simeon and knew if Benjamin died then the loss of three sons would be the death of him. Reuben even offers his own two children as a sacrifice if in fact Benjamin and Simeon did not return, but Jacob rejects his proposal. They are stuck with a limited amount of grain, a famine that held little relief and one brother stuck in jail in a foreign country. Things could not be worse for this band of brothers knowing all along the guilt of their past.

> **Genesis 43:1 Now the famine was severe in the land. So it came about when they had finished eating the grain which they had brought from Egypt, that their father said to them, "Go back, buy us a little food."**

Desperate situations force our hand sometimes. One too many blackouts after a night of drinking might mean it's time to join AA. A pain that won't go away might mean a trip to the doctor regardless of your fear of physicians. A relationship that is marred by abuse might need to end. Many times God will make sure we are at the end of our rope before He steps in and moves us to the place He needs us to be.

For Jacob, he realized he would know the pain of not only Joseph's supposed death but that of his entire family; children and grandchildren, as he realized they would die of starvation. At some point enough was enough and Jacob made the decision to allow Benjamin to go with his brothers to get more grain.

> **Genesis 43:11-15 Then their father Israel said to them, "If it must be so, then do this: take some of the best products of the land in your bags, and carry down to the man as a present, a little balm and a little honey, aromatic gum and myrrh, pistachio nuts and almonds. "Take double the money in your hand, and take back in your hand the money that was returned in the mouth of your sacks; perhaps it was a mistake. "Take your brother also, and arise, return to the man; and may God Almighty grant you compassion in the sight of the man, so that he will release to you your other brother**

> **and Benjamin. And as for me, if I am bereaved of my children, I am bereaved." So the men took this present, and they took double the money in their hand, and Benjamin; then they arose and went down to Egypt and stood before Joseph.**

What happens to Jacob is what needs to happen to us. We have to resign ourselves to God's plan for our lives. We have to do the best we can and leave the rest up to God to do what we can't. In our business we have days where we are at an impasse. We have worked diligently, we have put a budget together and sales calls are made. But when we know in three weeks that our company will be shut down if there is not an infusion of cash, we are able to sleep at night knowing we have done our best. Solomon says this in **Proverbs 21:31 "The horse is prepared for the day of battle, but victory belongs to the LORD."**

Our job is to work hard, go to school, study, and work with integrity. Our job is to put out applications if we need a job or start exercising if we need to lose weight. For you it might mean refusing to buy that extra bottle of alcohol, putting boundaries around what you watch on your computer or refusing to go places you know will cause you to stumble.

For Jacob, he had to release his son, his precious son from the only woman he ever loved, and allow him to go to Egypt regardless of the outcome. Many times for God to move, we have to let go first, which allows Him to do what needs to be done. Letting go proves to Him that we trust Him. The Amplified Bible says the word "trust" means: leaned on, relied on and confident in.

When we were down to $262.00 in our business, the word "trust" in the Amplified Bible brought new meaning. Suddenly we knew that our reliance could not be on people or circumstances but only on God. We prayed. We became confident in Him alone. We leaned on Him. And years later we can look back and say "we made it." Somehow God had provided every week for our business and many times it was miraculous. But through it all we learned that we had to do our part and let God do His.

Jacob finally changes his mind and allows Benjamin to go to Egypt and help rescue Simeon. Along with the money they found in their bags, they bring gifts in hope that favor would be bestowed upon them. It was time to come clean with this Egyptian man who held the future of their family in his hands. Unbeknownst to them, this man was their brother Joseph.

> **Genesis 43:16-23 When Joseph saw Benjamin with them, he said to his house steward, "Bring the men into the house, and slay an animal and make ready; for the men are to dine with me at noon." So the man did as Joseph said, and brought the men to Joseph's house. Now the men were afraid, because they were brought to Joseph's house; and they said, "It is because of the money that was returned in our sacks the first time that we are being brought in, that he may seek occasion against us and fall upon us, and take us for slaves with our donkeys."**
>
> **So they came near to Joseph's house steward, and spoke to him at the entrance of the house, and said, "Oh, my lord, we indeed came**

down the first time to buy food, and it came about when we came to the lodging place, that we opened our sacks, and behold, each man's money was in the mouth of his sack, our money in full. So we have brought it back in our hand. "We have also brought down other money in our hand to buy food; we do not know who put our money in our sacks." He said, "Be at ease, do not be afraid. Your God and the God of your father has given you treasure in your sacks; I had your money." Then he brought Simeon out to them.

Genesis 43:26-31 When Joseph came home, they brought into the house to him the present which was in their hand and bowed to the ground before him. Then he asked them about their welfare, and said, "Is your old father well, of whom you spoke? Is he still alive?" They said, "Your servant our father is well; he is still alive." They bowed down in homage. As he lifted his eyes and saw his brother Benjamin, his mother's son, he said, "Is this your youngest brother, of whom you spoke to me?" And he said, "May God be gracious to you, my son." Joseph hurried out for he was deeply stirred over his brother, and he sought a place to weep; and he entered his chamber and wept there. Then he washed his face and came out; and he controlled himself and said, "Serve the meal."

Joseph needed to know his brothers had changed. By putting the money in their sacks he wanted them to prove that they would come clean with the truth and the test worked. They told the house steward exactly what had happened. The brothers assumed they were in trouble but Joseph just wanted to see Benjamin and see how his father was.

When Joseph entered the room, his brothers bowed down to him. It must have been a bittersweet moment for him as he remembered his dream as a child once again. God was still in this whole situation and this was a great reminder that he was exactly where he was supposed to be.

God can restore anything. If you have a relationship that has gone bad, remember how God worked through all the bad in Joseph's life and then restored the bond with his brothers. Maybe for you it is a family member, an ex-spouse, a wayward child. Possibly it is a relationship with a best friend or a co-worker that has been broken apart. Yet God is a God of restoration and just like Joseph being restored to his family, you too can be the recipient of the same.

Joseph was overwhelmed by what was happening. He tested them and they came through. He wanted to see Benjamin and he was now in front of him. The men they were twenty years before were not the men in front of him now. The hatred was gone. The selfishness was gone. The pride was gone. They grew up. They remembered their sin. They were humble and because of this, Joseph was inundated with emotion. He walked out and burst into tears.

Joseph added God into the equation in his life and now he was reaping the benefits of trusting his heartbreaking relationships to God. His family was brought back to him and God can do the same for you. Start praying for the person who hurt you. Start asking God to arrange circumstances for reconciliation. After seeing the life of Joseph, we can be assured that God can do anything.

We have to decide if we have a big God and small problems or a small God and big problems. The more we grow in our faith, the more we learn about God, the bigger He becomes in our lives. If God created this world, gave us a heartbeat, made birds to fly and fish to swim – He can change the hearts of men and women.

For Joseph, it took years but it happened. Keep praying, keep trusting and keep waiting. God brings all things to fruition in His timing and in His way and it will happen in such a way that we know it was only Him. Joseph could never have orchestrated the events in his life to have such a dramatic reunion. Only God could do that and we need to know He can do the same for us.

Chapter 12

Forgiveness and Reconciliation

Joseph decides to test his brothers one last time before he reveals who he really is. He knows his brothers came back for Simeon because he was their blood brother but what about Benjamin? He was born to Joseph's mother Rachel. Did they love him less because he was a step brother? Would they walk away from him like they did to Joseph years before? Would they care for their father's feelings this time around with Benjamin's life at stake?

So, Joseph gives them one last test.

> **Genesis 44:1-13 Then he commanded his house steward, saying, "Fill the men's sacks with food, as much as they can carry, and put each man's money in the mouth of his sack. "Put my cup, the silver cup, in the mouth of the sack of the youngest, and his money for the grain." And he did as Joseph had told him. As soon as it was light, the men were sent away, they with their donkeys. They had just gone out of the city, and were not far off, when Joseph said to his house steward, "Up, follow the men; and when you overtake them, say to them, 'Why have you repaid evil for good? 'Is not this the one from which my lord drinks and which he indeed uses for divination? You have done wrong in doing**

this.' "So he overtook them and spoke these words to them. They said to him, "Why does my lord speak such words as these? Far be it from your servants to do such a thing. "Behold, the money which we found in the mouth of our sacks we have brought back to you from the land of Canaan. How then could we steal silver or gold from your lord's house? "With whomever of your servants it is found, let him die, and we also will be my lord's slaves." So he said, "Now let it also be according to your words; he with whom it is found shall be my slave, and the rest of you shall be innocent." Then they hurried, each man lowered his sack to the ground, and each man opened his sack. He searched, beginning with the oldest and ending with the youngest, and the cup was found in Benjamin's sack. Then they tore their clothes, and when each man loaded his donkey, they returned to the city.

Just when the brothers think all is well, they are overtaken and accused of stealing Joseph's silver cup, which of course they did not do. Joseph set this up to see their reaction and if they in fact would stand up for their younger step brother, Benjamin. They could not believe what was happening. Benjamin was in deep trouble and now the truth was about to come out regarding the loyalty of Joseph's brothers.

Genesis 44:14-17 When Judah and his brothers came to Joseph's house, he was still there, and they fell to the ground before him. Joseph said to them, "What is this deed that you have done? Do you not know that such a man as I

> **can indeed practice divination?" So Judah said, "What can we say to my lord? What can we speak? And how can we justify ourselves? God has found out the iniquity of your servants; behold, we are my lord's slaves, both we and the one in whose possession the cup has been found." But he said, "Far be it from me to do this. The man in whose possession the cup has been found, he shall be my slave; but as for you, go up in peace to your father."**

The integrity of his brothers was now on the line. This was the moment Joseph was waiting for. Would they leave Benjamin, alone in a foreign country, like they had done twenty years earlier to him? Or had they changed over the years? Would they take the grain and go home to their father? Would they lie their way out again without a thought or care for Benjamin?

> **Genesis 44:18-34 Then Judah approached him, and said, "Oh my lord, may your servant please speak a word in my lord's ears, and do not be angry with your servant; for you are equal to Pharaoh. "My lord asked his servants, saying, 'Have you a father or a brother?' "We said to my lord, 'We have an old father and a little child of his old age. Now his brother is dead, so he alone is left of his mother, and his father loves him.' "Then you said to your servants, 'Bring him down to me that I may set my eyes on him.' "But we said to my lord, 'The lad cannot leave his father, for if he should leave his father, his father would die.' "You said to your servants, however, 'Unless your youngest brother comes down with you, you will not**

see my face again.' "Thus it came about when we went up to your servant my father, we told him the words of my lord. "Our father said, 'Go back, buy us a little food.' "But we said, 'We cannot go down. If our youngest brother is with us, then we will go down; for we cannot see the man's face unless our youngest brother is with us.' "Your servant my father said to us, 'You know that my wife bore me two sons; and the one went out from me, and I said, "Surely he is torn in pieces," and I have not seen him since. 'If you take this one also from me, and harm befalls him, you will bring my gray hair down to Sheol in sorrow.' "Now, therefore, when I come to your servant my father, and the lad is not with us, since his life is bound up in the lad's life, when he sees that the lad is not with us, he will die. Thus your servants will bring the gray hair of your servant our father down to Sheol in sorrow. "For your servant became surety for the lad to my father, saying, 'If I do not bring him back to you, then let me bear the blame before my father forever.' "Now, therefore, please let your servant remain instead of the lad a slave to my lord, and let the lad go up with his brothers. "For how shall I go up to my father if the lad is not with me—for fear that I see the evil that would overtake my father?"

Finally the truth comes out for Joseph. His brothers do care. They had grown up. They were not the selfish men they were twenty years before. Judah was willing to give his life up for Benjamin in order to keep him safe. This was the moment Joseph had been waiting for and he could not keep his secret a minute more.

Genesis 45:1-8 Then Joseph could not control himself before all those who stood by him, and he cried, "Have everyone go out from me." So there was no man with him when Joseph made himself known to his brothers. He wept so loudly that the Egyptians heard it, and the household of Pharaoh heard of it. Then Joseph said to his brothers, "I am Joseph! Is my father still alive?" But his brothers could not answer him, for they were dismayed at his presence. Then Joseph said to his brothers, "Please come closer to me." And they came closer. And he said, "I am your brother Joseph, whom you sold into Egypt. "Now do not be grieved or angry with yourselves, because you sold me here, for God sent me before you to preserve life. "For the famine has been in the land these two years, and there are still five years in which there will be neither plowing nor harvesting. "God sent me before you to preserve for you a remnant in the earth, and to keep you alive by a great deliverance. "Now, therefore, it was not you who sent me here, but God; and He has made me a father to Pharaoh and lord of all his household and ruler over all the land of Egypt.

As they stood there speechless, fear, guilt, shame and shock must have been what these men were feeling. They could not believe what they were hearing and yet what probably amazed them the most was Joseph's attitude. No hatred or bitterness. No throwing them in prison. No anger for what they did to him. But what they heard was something they could never fathom: grace, mercy, kindness and God.

A God perspective! Joseph was able to look at his life and recognize God at the heart of his last twenty years. He understood that even his brothers' hatred of him was part of God's plan to save Israel and Egypt. His prison time and the false accusation against him all fell under the umbrella of God being added into the equation.

Now let's look at our own lives. Think how different we would be if we could trust God's hand in all our situations. And because Joseph did we can see how he handles his brothers – first with an accusation, then with forgiveness and finally giving all the glory to God.

You sold me into Egypt.
Do not be angry with yourselves.
God used you to send me here.
God sent me to preserve your life.
You did not send me here,
BUT GOD DID!

And yet our problem is that we want things to go our way now. We don't want to spend twenty years waiting for restoration. We don't want to wait for God's perfect timing because His timing seems like forever. And yet for Joseph and his brothers, in the proper time – twenty years later – God restored his family back to himself. So if something in your life seems like it will never happen, remember Joseph. Remember that his job was to refuse bitterness and hatred. His job was to do his very best each day where God had placed him regardless if he wanted to be there or not. Joseph did the right things, had the right attitude, and God blessed him in the end with his entire family moving to Egypt.

Genesis 45:9-15 "Hurry and go up to my father, and say to him, 'Thus says your son Joseph, "God has made me lord of all Egypt; come down to me, do not delay. "You shall live in the land of Goshen, and you shall be near me, you and your children and your children's children and your flocks and your herds and all that you have. "There I will also provide for you, for there are still five years of famine to come, and you and your household and all that you have would be impoverished." ' "Behold, your eyes see, and the eyes of my brother Benjamin see, that it is my mouth which is speaking to you. "Now you must tell my father of all my splendor in Egypt, and all that you have seen; and you must hurry and bring my father down here." Then he fell on his brother Benjamin's neck and wept, and Benjamin wept on his neck. He kissed all his brothers and wept on them, and afterward his brothers talked with him.

What a way to end a story.

Grace – I know what you did to me but I am past it.

Forgiveness – I know what you did to me but I won't remember it.

Reconciliation – I know what you did to me but I am so thankful to have you back in my life.

Kindness – I know what you did to me but I want to take care of you the rest of your life.

That is what happens when we add God into the equations of our lives. We have a different perspective. We see things differently than most people. We see all that happens through the filter of God and what His plans are for us. For Joseph, he modeled this to perfection for us and through his story we are able to see the faithfulness of God. He works through pain and hardship. His timing never seems soon enough. And yet, seeing how Joseph ends his life gives us the hope we need for our lives.

What God did for Joseph, He can do for us. We just need to add Him to our equation.

As the story of Joseph concludes, we see how God blesses those who trust Him. Joseph never wavered in his commitment to doing the right thing. He never hesitated to be all God asked of him even in the darkest hours of his life. This is how his story continues.

> **Genesis 45:16-28 Now when the news was heard in Pharaoh's house that Joseph's brothers had come, it pleased Pharaoh and his servants. Then Pharaoh said to Joseph, "Say to your brothers, 'Do this: load your beasts and go to the land of Canaan, and take your father and your households and come to me, and I will give you the best of the land of Egypt and you will eat the fat of the land.' "Now you are ordered, 'Do this: take wagons from the land of Egypt for your little ones and for your wives, and bring your father and come. 'Do not concern yourselves with your goods, for the best of all the land of Egypt is yours.' " Then the sons of Israel did so; and Joseph gave them**

> **wagons according to the command of Pharaoh, and gave them provisions for the journey. To each of them he gave changes of garments, but to Benjamin he gave three hundred pieces of silver and five changes of garments. To his father he sent as follows: ten donkeys loaded with the best things of Egypt, and ten female donkeys loaded with grain and bread and sustenance for his father on the journey. So he sent his brothers away, and as they departed, he said to them, "Do not quarrel on the journey." Then they went up from Egypt, and came to the land of Canaan to their father Jacob. They told him, saying, "Joseph is still alive, and indeed he is ruler over all the land of Egypt." But he was stunned, for he did not believe them. When they told him all the words of Joseph that he had spoken to them, and when he saw the wagons that Joseph had sent to carry him, the spirit of their father Jacob revived. Then Israel said, "It is enough; my son Joseph is still alive. I will go and see him before I die."**

Because of Joseph's position, Pharaoh was pleased to help in any way needed to bring Joseph's family to Egypt. Joseph was allowed to take wagons, provisions, animals, grain and bread for the trip. Imagine how Jacob, his father, must have felt when the caravan showed up in Canaan! Once he heard his long lost son, presumed to be dead, was actually alive the Bible says "the spirit of their father was revived."

What a time for the family. What a time of renewal for a once dysfunctional family that finally grew up, confessed their sin, became honest, and learned from their past mistakes. All of this was done because God had a plan many years before for Joseph to save their country from famine and it took the heartaches of life to allow him the opportunity.

Here are some additional blessings:

> **Genesis 46:2-4 God spoke to Israel in visions of the night and said, "Jacob, Jacob." And he said, "Here I am." He said, "I am God, the God of your father; do not be afraid to go down to Egypt, for I will make you a great nation there. "I will go down with you to Egypt, and I will also surely bring you up again; and Joseph will close your eyes." Then Jacob arose from Beersheba; and the sons of Israel carried their father Jacob and their little ones and their wives in the wagons which Pharaoh had sent to carry him.**

God comforted Jacob, reassuring him that a great nation would be built out of his offspring and he would die with Joseph by his side.

> **Genesis 47:6 "The land of Egypt is at your disposal; settle your father and your brothers in the best of the land, let them live in the land of Goshen; and if you know any capable men among them, then put them in charge of my livestock."**

Pharaoh would give the best land in Egypt to Joseph's family and give them a job.

Think how Joseph must have felt as he looked out at the family he thought he lost forever. He could see how awesome God was and now looking back over his life, he now saw the purpose in his pain. We need to recognize that God does the same for us.

Problem +Pain+God = Healing

Chapter 13

God Meant it For Good

As we see the conclusion to the life of Joseph, we are reminded of how different our lives can be if we add God into our equations. What we see is the grace Joseph has all the way to the end. After seventeen years of living in Egypt with his family, Joseph's father died with his family close by. With the passing of his life, suddenly Joseph's brothers became fearful for their lives. Somehow in their mind they began to convince themselves that Joseph was only being kind to them because of their father.

> **Genesis 50:15-18 When Joseph's brothers saw that their father was dead, they said, "What if Joseph bears a grudge against us and pays us back in full for all the wrong which we did to him!" So they sent a message to Joseph, saying, "Your father charged before he died, saying, 'Thus you shall say to Joseph, "Please forgive, I beg you, the transgression of your brothers and their sin, for they did you wrong." ' And now, please forgive the transgression of the servants of the God of your father." And Joseph wept when they spoke to him. Then his brothers also came and fell down before him and said, "Behold, we are your servants."**

It seems that Joseph was saddened by his brothers' fear. The forgiveness he had extended to them was never based on his father being alive but was based on his God. God had restored his family and Joseph would never allow unforgiveness to enter his life. He had added God into this equation many years before and to Joseph, the past had been forgotten.

Joseph had a great message for his brothers and one that could change our perspective on life if we truly lived by it. Here is what he said:

> **Genesis 50:19-21 But Joseph said to them, "Do not be afraid, for am I in God's place? As for you, you meant evil against me, but God meant it for good in order to bring about this present result, to preserve many people alive. So therefore, do not be afraid; I will provide for you and your little ones." So he comforted them and spoke kindly to them.**

Remember this:

What someone meant evil against you, God can use it for good.

Think if we could actually live our lives with this as our motto. Yes, you hurt me but my God will use it for good. Yes, bad situations have come into my life that seem evil but my God will use it for good. Every day when things change, always remember how Joseph lived his life with this thought. He moved through life trusting that God had a purpose behind all the hurt and pain and we see how God blessed his life for that.

Joseph ended well. He provided for his family who hurt him. He spoke kindly to them. He cared for their feelings and their fears. He was reassuring, loving and forgiving. And he did this because he spent his life under the protection of God. He took the storms in his life and added God into his equation and because of that we see his outcome: peace.

Joseph lived in peace even though the storms were raging all around him. As the winds of deception and pain tried to destroy him, he would not let them because with God added into his equation, he knew God had a plan. Joseph's job would be to wait and trust and that is what we can learn from his life. He waited for years and God took him from a prison to a palace. He trusted God and was given his family back. He weathered the storms under the shelter of the only covering he knew – his trust that God knew exactly what He was doing with his life.

Always remember:

> ME + PROBLEMS = FRUSTRATION AND TURMOIL
>
> ME + PROBLEMS + GOD = PEACE

And the situation we told you about in the first chapter that moved us to write this book? After years of wondering why God would allow such heartache in the life of someone close to us, God has graciously redeemed the situation with a wonderful addition to us all. Looking back we can see how much Joseph taught us – that if we would add God into the situation and leave vengeance up to Him – He could do something great. We learned our own valuable lessons and are grateful for the shining example of Joseph that helped us through some very difficult days.

And in the end, we know this book would never have been written if this situation had not come into our lives. As we look over the past few years, just like Joseph did, we can see the hand of God through it all and what someone meant for evil, God has used for good.

May Joseph's life be an example to us that as we add God to every equation, we will recognize He has a purpose and plan, even in the midst of our most difficult days.

Always remember that me plus my problem plus God will equal peace.

If you have any questions or comments,
please e-mail us at:

Lisa@WomensBibleStudy.com
or
robslaizure@gmail.com

Visit us at our website:
ConnectingTheDotsMinistries.com